"Winston Churchill was a Catholic Priest"

Memoirs from Thirty-Seven Years as a Public High School Teacher

---

by
Richard Doyle

authorHOUSE®

AuthorHouse™
1663 Liberty Drive, Suite 200
Bloomington, IN 47403
www.authorhouse.com
Phone: 1-800-839-8640

This book is a work of non-fiction. Unless otherwise noted, the author
and the publisher make no explicit guarantees as to the accuracy of
the information contained in this book and in some cases, names of
people and places have been altered to protect their privacy.

First published by AuthorHouse 11/25/2008

ISBN: 978-1-4389-1294-3 (sc)

Library of Congress Control Number: 2008908422

Printed in the United States of America
Bloomington, Indiana

This book is printed on acid-free paper.

INTRODUCTION

What has happened to teachers and students over the past thirty years, in and out of the classroom? "Winston Churchill Was a Catholic Priest" is a humorous, sad, unique, and poignant collection of true teaching episodes that happened to a high school teacher in New England over that period of time and more. As a social studies and theater arts educator, he has seen and heard it all. Being president of the teachers' association for the last four years of his career provided a keen insight into circumstances that only teachers could experience and have to deal with directly.

Funny occurrences like late-to-class excuses and off-the- wall classroom remarks only teenagers could make are included. Unrealistic demands on teachers and parental expectations make for unique reading. Crazy answers to test questions—from whence the book's title came— provide understanding into what makes a typical public high school what it is today.

Teachers will relate immediately, and the general public will learn much of what makes public schools tick. You will learn about teachers in kindergarden through twelfth grade as dedicated instructors who put up with way too much and never say "no " to anything except when administrators go too far and teachers have to stand up for their rights and their students' future.

"*Winston Churchill Was a Catholic Priest*" is a fast-paced read about a career of a man who persevered through it all, from challenging kids to challenging authorities. For everybody in schools today and everyone who ever went to school, this non-fiction story will strike you as compelling as it is real.

In some instances, names have been changed to protect the privacy of people in the book.

DEDICATION ────────────────────────

To my mother who wanted to be a teacher, to my sister who was trained as a teacher and to my wife who was a teacher.

ACKNOWLEDGEMENTS ─────────────

This book would not have been published without the help & assistance of

Neil Schulman of "Get Between the Covers" for his support.

The incredible staff at *www.authorhouse.com.* especially

Dylan Stanton for his initial assistance, Joel Pierson for his great proofreading knowledge, Bob DeGroff for his wonderful guidance & patience in actual publication & Jessica Sheese for her enthusiasm & encouragement.

Megan Little, for her invaluable assistant in the final stages of production.

William Bennett, former Secretary of Education, for giving permission to use the article on fine arts.

All my unique students over the years who were the inspiration for this book.

My terrific teaching colleagues who lived so much of this book with me-you are the best!

My wife, Barbara, for all the little & big things with which she helped me.

Some material in chapters 10 & 11 appeared in the Newburyport Daily News.

TABLE OF CONTENTS

Just like inside the world of education, the chapters headings sometimes relate to what you will find in that chapter and sometimes they just relate to things that happened totally out of the blue!

CHAPTER 1
Does Spelling Count?

The way most schools are built today, it seems they have miles of straight corridors. You walk forever and it takes a long time get to your destination, because you can see how far away it is. Corridors seem like wasted space but what's the solution? In my old school, which was built in the shape of a "U," the corridors did not seem to go on forever, and it was actually better because you'd never know who or what was coming around the corner!

Such was my teaching career. It was like the corridors that you'd walk through to get to where you were headed, but not knowing who or what was coming around the corner in education with the latest schemes to revolutionize practically everything. Basically, learning is really quite simple—the teacher produces material that the student must learn. There's no trick to it. Just sit down and do your class work and your homework and you'll be fine. It's everything else that gets in the way for the players—the teachers and the kids.

I taught for thirty-seven years in a small New England community that tried many times to find itself, and in turn, the schools had to catch up with the community whose kids we were serving. This stretched from the volatile sixties to the new millennium. I usually had great cooperation from parents back in the beginning, but I found more resistance from some parents toward the end of my career Somewhere along the line, it seemed that parents almost became too involved in schools for many different reasons. They didn't know enough about what teachers were trying to do except as it affected their children. Many times they approached the school administration and get their voices heard. This is long before we are even asked to voice ours. One thing seemed to get lost in the shuffle was that we were all in it for the same thing- the kids!

Kids provide humor every day—sometimes without even knowing it. I always loved the excuses they used to write on the tardy slips for reasons they would give for being late to school, like:

"Moose in backyard." I was so taken aback by this one, I requested that the boy see me after school. He explained that he was late because a live moose came out of the woods and was running around the neighborhood. I asked him if he expected me to believe that! Later, when I got home and was watching the evening news, lo and behold—it was showing a moose in a backyard of our city, and the boy was telling the truth.

Another one—"Dunkin' Donuts line to long," with "too" spelled wrong.

Another one—"I don't know." At least he was honest!

Another one—"Had to take prom tux back." The shop is only open until 5 PM and school gets out at 2:00!

When I graduated from college in June of 1965, I did not have job. When the beginning of August rolled around, I did not have a job. Most of my friends had settled for teaching positions in New Hampshire, where most of them were from—but not me. I wanted to teach in my home state of Massachusetts, mainly because teacher salaries were much better there. So I held out, and it looked like I might not have a job come September.

One rainy Saturday afternoon, I remember sitting in my den and banging away at my old college typewriter, completing thirty-seven teaching applications. These ranged all over New England to New York State. Nothing came through, but finally it boiled down to two school systems, one in my hometown (where I vowed never to teach) and one in a neighboring system.

I received a call for an interview at the nearby school system and went. There was another fellow there at the interview with me, and it became apparent that we were the final candidates for the position. As the superintendent asked one then the other the same question, I vowed that once this ended—even if I was the successful candidate—I would never teach there. Besides, it was for a junior high world history job, and I wanted my first love, American history or nothing.

When I got home from the interview, in the mail came a letter from my hometown's high school principal. He wanted to see me about an American history post! Well, maybe I could teach in my hometown after all—if nothing else came through.

I went for the interview and was referred to the superintendent's office after the high school principal said that the job was mine if I wanted it. The old superintendent who was still there when I was a student was a gruff veteran of World War II who was known for brevity and lack of people skills. He was very short and sweet that morning, and as the interview concluded, he said something to me that carried me my whole teaching career. He said, "You going to teach history?" I replied, "Yes, sir." He retorted with, "Well, you better be interesting!" That became my motivating commandment for my entire thirty-seven-year career. If I didn't like the subject and was boring, how could my students learn? I always tried to be interesting.

My students liked to come to my class, I learned from time to time. "We always do something in here," they often remarked. This really took me aback more than once, so one day I asked them what they meant. They told me that one of their teachers was absent and had left no plans, and while another teacher was in, since it was Monday, she hadn't prepared anything over the weekend for them. I was appalled! I, who used to write my "script" every night from the textbook and made intricate lesson plans each day, was flabbergasted. How could someone like that call herself a teacher?

CHAPTER 2
I Don't Have a Thing to Write With

Teachers come in all shapes and sizes and varied backgrounds. They are unique for what they represent as people with a calling to teach young people. The kids think we were all valedictorians; how far from the truth that was! Many people I taught with had very hard knocks to overcome while obtaining their education.

My own personal background was very different from the norm. My parents were divorced since I was six years old. I had no male role model around, as my valiant mother struggled to raise me and my sister. We had a wonderful maternal family that was such a inspiration to us. It was composed of educators mostly, and that is were I got my desire to teach, I am sure. My uncles were superintendents of schools and high school principals. Aunts and cousins were teachers, so I had very good roles models to emulate.

Some of my fellow teachers were "other things" before they stepped into the classroom. One woman had a family of seven children before she taught. She was valedictorian of her high school class and became a wife and mother first then went on to get her college degree afterward. She was just a dynamo, and became my department chair eventually. She was very "hyper" and constantly on the go from dawn to dusk. She was also very fair and open when evaluating us. She helped one teacher after another to do the very best job we could, and saw to it that we had the latest in supplies with which to do it.

Public schools must adhere to state guidelines of a certain number of hours and days they must be open in order to receive state financial aid. In Massachusetts, the law was changed in 1993 to have high schools meet at least 990 hours for instruction. How the local communities decide to do this is entirely up to them. In Newburyport, the high school day used to start at 8 AM and end at 2:20 PM until 1993. Then it was changed to start at 7:30 AM and end at 2:05 PM. This is roughly six and a half hours a day, and it was insane! To think of teaching teenagers that early after the majority of them have worked until 11:00 PM or later at gas stations or fast-food eateries is crazy. No one is awake that early—let alone ready to learn. I always faced kids who were asleep in front of me when this schedule was incorporated. Added to this was a brilliant idea to increase class length from a manageable forty-five minutes daily to ninety minutes every other day! Where do these people get off? Teenagers are itchy, fidgety kids. To even think that they could stay tuned to anything for an hour and a half is indeed totally irrational.

Many times over the years, I have learned not to use names of real students when giving examples, for they take it to heart or misunderstand that I was only using "Lisa" or "Tim" to gain their attention. So I thought up names no one in our school was ever named, so I could still bring a student name to my point. I relied on "Ethel" and "Leroy" and made my points—many times evoking a laugh from the class as an added bonus for using these names.

Sometimes kids act like jerks, especially when the temperature gets hot and it's time to bring in floor fans from my home to cool off the classroom. Invariably, kids want to sit right in front of it to hog all the cool air for themselves. I usually tried to keep the fan near me in the front of the room, to keep myself cool while teaching. It wasn't anything special, usually the oscillating type that made its way to the classroom for eighty-five-degree and hotter days. Once, a real jerk actually sat *on* the fan, and that was the end of it. I yelled at him, since I was primarily concerned with safety, and I pulled the damn plug out. When putting it away in the coat closet, I informed the class that they would have to sweat because this kid couldn't behave. You'd think they never saw a fan or had one at their own home—maybe they didn't, for all I know!

I taught for years on the third floor of the high school, in a room that overlooked the parking lot adjacent to the gym. While pacing back and forth, instructing my classes, I often glanced out the window and watched physical education classes go to and fro on the athletic field, located a short distance from the building. Escorting classes to this location, the teacher had a couple of students who led the classes. On one such occasion, as this group scurried to the field, the male gym teacher yelled to the kids, "Hey girls, have you got balls?" That pretty much did it for me and the senior boys in the back of my room. All concentration was lost, and I quickly finished my point and sat down laughing. The class proceeded to start on the assignment I gave them for homework!

Occasionally, a teacher gets a superior student in class whose test answers to essay questions are so good, it is really like reading a book. Such a student was Bob, who I had the good fortune to encounter in my very first year as a history teacher. I couldn't wait to get to his papers, because they made all the others I had to plow more bearable. His

7

command of the English language for a mere high school sophomore was indeed remarkable. Needless to say, he got straight As in the course, and when he took the SATs he attained perfect 800s on both the verbal and math portions of the aptitude test. To no one's surprise—least of all mine—he graduated six years later from Harvard!

While directing a show once, I asked the actor to turn around in a counter clockwise direction and she did it wrong repeatedly.

So I asked her "What's the problem? Don't you know what that means?"

She replied, "I have a digital watch!"

CHAPTER 3
Hey, Teacher, He Just Hit Me!

Who goes into teaching? I met some wonderful people in this profession, and I worked with some truly unique individuals. There was the teacher who dressed as a drum majorette sometimes, and she didn't teach music! One fellow defied authorities in the '60s by not saluting the flag, and showed up in dungarees and wearing a beard. He later wound up in court for his outrageous views! One girl thought it would be cute to have her students call her by her first name. Soon this idea reached the teachers' room, and a well-respected grand dame put this young thing in her place by explaining very calmly that there wasn't much left in this profession for teachers, and once we lost the Miss or Mister labels from our students, we have lost everything. The air was thick with stress in the room; thank God the bell rang and we all very gingerly made our way to class!

I met very few good administrators in thirty-seven years. I worked under five principals and two interim principals. They forget what its like for the teacher once they become administrators. They seem to forget that the title of principal means nothing but "main teacher in the school." Unfortunately, today principals are buried in their offices, secluded from the staff and kids. I truly believe that every principal and superintendent should teach at least one course, one semester, each school year. The head of the American Medical Association doesn't stop operating, does he? No, he continues to practice, just like the head judge of the American Bar Association doesn't stop hearing court cases. Education is the only profession that isolates its leaders in little offices, away from the classroom, once they are appointed principal. They lose contact very quickly, and they forget from whence they came, for the most part. If they taught a course—at any level—they would least have to put up with what teachers deal with daily: namely unruly students, special ed. dictums, and unreasonable parents. Some states should take the lead and require administrators to teach. If there is too much paperwork presently, then cut the paperwork. Cut the meetings and demands from outside that are ruining public education today.

For the most part, I got along with the students I taught over the years. Once in a while, I had to really delve into their psyches and to understand why we weren't clicking. Sometimes personality clashes occur in the teaching profession; that is inevitable. I was having a problem a few years ago with a very immature teenage boy who was always late to class and sought distractions while in class. This went on for a while, and finally I asked him to stay after class so I could talk to him. Once everyone had left, we sat down and I asked, "What's the problem? Is it me? Are you like this in other classes? What can we do to make for a better relationship?" Finally, after a brief silence, he said, "Mr. Doyle, all I do is think about sex and music all day!" *In that order,* I said to myself! Thinking quickly, I responded with, "Well, that won't help you pass my course, so I suggest that you try to get your homework done."

He then asked if I wanted to see his snake tattoo. "It goes all the way up my leg" he said and proceeded to roll up his pant cuff. I told him that was all right I'd take his word for it. "How much did that cost you? "I asked. Four hundred dollars, He said. My God, I thought, these kids really get ripped off don't they?

During my very first year of teaching, while correcting my first midyear exams, I saw that a student had written an answer to a test question that I never forgot. While identifying world leaders from a list of ten or fifteen that among others included Winston Churchill, she put down that he was a Catholic priest! In the same pile of papers, one student identified General Electric as a Confederate general in the Civil War. You must understand that I always encouraged students to guess rather than leave an item blank. They might get it right and score a few points. In these cases, I couldn't give a single point to either student. Years later, I spotted the first girl downtown, pushing a baby carriage, with another in tow, probably still having no idea that Sir Winston provided a lot in World War II with his superb leadership that allowed her to be a mother and enjoy the freedom that our soldiers fought for so gallantly, but having absolutely nothing to do with the priesthood!

In order to contribute to the overall atmosphere of the school, teachers are quite often asked to get involved in extracurricular activities that range from class or club advisorships to the coaching of a sport. I was active in college on yearbook and theatre, so it was natural for me to lean in those directions. For eight years, I advised rather good yearbooks, and for seventeen years, I produced and directed plays and musicals. Once, while in the middle of a very quick backstage costume change, a girl asked me to hook her bra for her, which I did, and on she went to perform a dance number. Today, I would never have done it, since laws are so touchy regarding contact with students, but back then, who knew? Also, the arts enable teachers and students to work toward a common goal—production of a show. Too often, however, the arts are the first to be cut in a budget crunch. Are they frivolous? I never thought so; rather, they contribute significantly to students' education. Kids like to see teachers out of the classroom in other environments. When I worked on plays, students saw me engaging in something other than book learning, and to show up on a Saturday in dungarees to paint scenery with them was always a great experience.

Unfortunately, not every student can be trusted as much as you might think. Students who work in the front office usually were sterling characters, assisting secretaries with messages to be taken or errands to run. Once, however, a student got into the handwritten report cards located in the main office and changed her D to a B. I never would have known, but at the parents' night open house, her mother commented on how pleased she was with her daughter's work in my class. I was taken aback and told the parent that her child received a D from me; how could she be happy with a grade like that if she was anticipating applying to college? The mother insisted that she saw a B on the report card and asked what I was talking about. After the conversation ended, I made my way to the office and pulled the report card out. Sure enough, there was the B, but upon close inspection, I discovered that the student had drawn in a little line in black ink to change the letter. The next day, I confronted the girl, who burst into tears and said that she couldn't go out Saturday nights if her mother ever found out what she had done. I told her that honesty was the best policy and that I would contact her mother, which I did, and set the situation right. The next quarter, the student did manage to pull a C grade and passed the course. I am sure she enjoyed many a Saturday night out after that!

CHAPTER 4 ———————————
Can I Have a Pass to the Nurse?

Part of the experience in theatre arts was producing the shows for a high school cast and audience. The first musical I did was Rodgers and Hammerstein's *South Pacific*, with a dynamic elementary music teacher. I was in charge of the scenery and most of the behind-the-scenes part of the production. Did I know what I was getting myself in for? No, but I wanted to do it and went ahead anyway.

South Pacific is a wonderful show with wonderful songs, and everyone knew it. One thing no one knew was that it contained twenty-five scenes in two acts that required some elaborate sets. Our stage was very small at the high school, so I had designed a lot of movable, revolving pieces that could be used two or three times differently. I involved a lot of people for this first production, like ticket sellers, costume gatherers, and makeup folk. I lined up the industrial arts teacher to actually build the scenery, except for the backdrops, which we rented from Boston. Well, everything seemed to be on schedule, except for the fact that the teacher knew nothing about stage work; he built the sets to last, out of very heavy materials. The walls of the units were made of very heavy sheetrock, which weighs a great deal and requires a lot of people to move or lift. We also needed to change scenery quickly in order to speed up the production, but found out at dress rehearsal just how heavy these things were when we couldn't exactly roll them off without ten or more kids lending a hand!

I spent a horrid evening at dress rehearsal and until 2 AM at home, rethinking the entire production. Finally, after much work, I developed a working chart that no one told me I would need, to make sure everything moved on and off pretty much like a choreographed production number. We had scenery by the yard and stored everywhere backstage, so it required great organization on my part. Naturally, the kids were wonderful, but much pre-planning was necessary before I told them what to do and how to do it so they could take bows before their parents for how hard they worked! Most audience members don't realize the tremendous work involved when they witness a two-hour production, whether it be Broadway or simply high school.

South Pacific contains a wonderful song about the heroine, Nellie Forbush, washing that man right out of her hair—on stage—live before the audience! To do this, we rigged up a small unit containing a shower with a garden hose and bucket to douse her head and shampoo in. At the infamous dress rehearsal, the young lady playing Nellie used too much shampoo, and we had lather everywhere. During the scene change, despite two hair dryers backstage, it was quite impossible for her to get her locks even semi-dry. As the production advanced for three nights, we had her just wash the front bangs of her hairdo, and that gave the same impression to the audience that the great Mary Martin did nightly on Broadway in the 1950s—except that Miss Martin had cut her hair very short, which helped greatly. Our star had long, flowing locks instead.

Certainly, the saddest part of being president of the Newburyport Teachers Association—which I was for the last four years of my career—was listening to someone who had just been told that his or her job was terminated. Under the Education Reform Act of 1993 in Massachusetts, teachers under professional status (less than three years' experience) can be let go without being given a reason if their release is within the first ninety days of their employment. We do not want bad teachers in the profession, but even Wal-Mart employees are at least told why they are being let go! Teachers can never improve if they can't be given a reason for termination. One such teacher sat with me for an hour and a half the day after she was informed that she had lost her job. I met with her in our association office during my free block and went the entire 360 degrees over the situation, the law, and her course of action. This poor girl was in her early twenties and could not comprehend what she had done wrong. I explained that she could resign, and then it wouldn't look so bad for further employment, but she really didn't think she wanted to be in education if this could happen. I sympathized with her entirely and provided a shoulder to cry on, because there wasn't much else I could do for her. We talked and talked, and finally she said that she would resign, and she thanked me for my help. I was just drained and I had a class waiting. To this day, I never did learn the true reason why she was terminated.

Professional development is this thing the administration thrust upon teachers to justify their own jobs—not the teachers'. Teachers are certainly busy enough without attending these ridiculous meetings once a month in order to keep up in the profession. Usually, "experts" from outside the classroom are brought at great expense to the school system to have teachers go to workshops when school is out of session. Administrators probably attended a conference or read an article in an education journal and saw great need to bring these folks to their system.

Kids are released once a month or teachers have to go an extra day or two to attend these things. To make it more acceptable, teachers are sometimes recruited to be in on the planning, but mostly it's the administrators who plan who the speakers will be and how the sessions will be run. They have to do something to justify the exorbitant amount of money they get paid! Methods and ideas are exchanged that teachers are expected to incorporate into their already-crowded curricula. Sometimes teachers must present evidence that they actually did what they were exposed to, and are even evaluated on these things. Much better use of professional time would be to have teachers meet and exchange ideas with others in the system who teach their subject or grade. Very little time is spent on this idea, and one really wonders why not.

In the 1960s and before, teachers' conventions were held each fall, but no one went. Local communities adopted their own early-release days to provide this wonderful professional-development opportunity that no likes. Mentally, no one goes either, but administrators still try to pretend that they are needed. What teachers really want is time to work together on curriculum that is in place and should be honed to finer expertise every educator has already.

Field trips are those wonderful experiences where kids and teachers get out of school to visit subject-related places. Organization is a headache that no teacher really needs, but we put up with it to help the kids have this experience. Money has to be collected for the bus, since it isn't in the school budget to provide transportation. Permission slips have to be obtained from all teachers whose classes the kids will miss, and parents need to okay their darlings' absence for the day. When the day arrives and the destination is reached, one big part of the experience is making sure that everyone is with you on the trip home. I had the unfortunate experience to leave a teenager behind on one such field trip. It wasn't until I got home and the phone rang during supper that a girl told me she was left behind and that her parent had to go and pick her up. If the child had stayed with the group, and if I had been more vigilant, it might not have happened. The point is, a teacher must be ever-organized and aware that high school kids can get lost just like younger children. Luckily, nothing dangerous came out of it. I took fewer field trips for this reason as the years went by.

Arsenic and Old Lace is a classic of the American theatre that I had my students perform one fall. The delightful story of two eccentric sisters who poison their tenants with elderberry wine, all the while putting up with a demented brother who thinks he's Teddy Roosevelt, never failed to be a comedy hit every time is was performed in the USA. During our production, we had a doorknob fall off the set, a lack of a much-needed pen as a prop, and the smashing of a kid's head into the set. It all made for a memorable show that ranks very high in my memory of "yes it is all worth it despite problems" of live theatre!

CHAPTER 5 ————————
Can I Go to the Bathroom?

Certainly there is no higher honor that can be given to a teacher than to be recognized by his students. This happened to me in 1974, when the school's yearbook was dedicated to me. I had advised eight staffs in my career, but this group of kids was among the very best. They were just so cooperative to work with, and an overall great class. Yearbook advising is just like having a sixth class. There is a tremendous amount of work and uphill struggle. Some schools run it as a class, but we always had it as an extracurricular activity.

This honor, coming less than ten years into my career, was a shot in the arm and something I treasured throughout my teaching adventure. I was kept in the dark about the accolade for a long time, but eventually, as advisor, I found out about it. It was still a very emotional time as I accepted the honor at the senior banquet that year. Closing my speech by quoting Carol Burnett, the TV comedienne, I told them that "I was so glad we had this time together!" And I meant every word of it.

This wonderful class still invites me to their class reunions, and it is great seeing them as adults with careers and families.

Whatever happened to school activities and fun after school?

I used to survey my college-level students each year, and out of an average class of twenty-five students, only four didn't have job after school or on weekends! Kids have to be kids. They will work the rest of their lives. Are finances so hard today that students must work daily after school instead of just during the summer, as we did?

I can remember getting a job at Christmas during my senior year to pay for class pictures, but I was very active in school and loved school activities. I worked each summer, and of course, during my college years, but not during high school.

We have a real problem with students being too tired and too busy to get involved in school activities. I believe after-school jobs are a big reason why! Now, I am certainly not as naive as it may seem. I do fully realize that a college education is frightfully expensive compared to when I was a student. I also realize that most households have two parents working full time, but must their children work too? And must they work to the extent that they do? Child labor was outlawed years ago. Schools were invented to teach kids to get ready to go into the workaday world after high school—not *during* high school. This generation of students is being robbed of one of the most precious times of their lives: adolescence. They will have nothing to look back on or to remember but he drudgery of work, labor, and employment.

I don't have the answer, and I know that in many ways, jobs teach kids the value of earning a salary and the work ethic, but I do not believe that we are doing the kids any good at all when we force or encourage them to get a job in the middle of the afternoon.

One may argue that it would do the students no good to hang around after school and get into trouble. Others may say that they are lucky to be able to work. To those arguments I also agree, but if the student in front of me is having trouble with the subject I am teaching and is too tired to perform in school to the best of his ability, then I feel that something is radically wrong when these kids are working too early.

I WAS JUST THINKING ...
—I'd rather have no chalk than have to write on the board with the cheap, breakable white stuff.
—Students who are habitually late to school will always be late to everything in life.
—Where are the parents you really want to see at parents' nights?
—Why do we have to feed students at lunch in any school cafeteria?
—Has anyone ever tried just marking everything that is right on a test paper, rather than marking the things that are wrong?
—Do students eat at home the way they do in the cafeteria?
—Why do elementary teachers talk like their students?
—Why don't retired teachers ever return, even just to visit?
—Students you always see in the hall always see you in the hall!
—Just what does cooperative learning really do?
—How long does it take to know all students' names each year?
—Name three of your students who could pass a test you gave ten years ago.
—How long does it take a substitute teacher to dress when called in the morning to come in?
—Educators with the most degrees never have the answer to anything.
—Do you dare tell your worst students that education is lifelong learning?
—What are we really doing for the average student?
—How many men teachers ever wear sport coats anymore?
—Acting lessons should be required as part of basic teacher training.
—Who's the last one out of school each day?

—Could school open if all the office secretaries were out on the same day?

—When will the "back-to-basics" movement return?

—Can any teacher watch a TV show dealing with school once they're home?

—Are earrings on boys really here to stay?

—How much pain do students endure with body piercing and tattoos when they scream about so much homework being assigned?

—Shouldn't the school library be open at night?

—It's too bad all those people who really know how to run this country are too busy teaching school!

—Attending class reunions as guests shows that we did a pretty good job after all is said and done!

CHAPTER 6

Please Encourage but Do Not Force Your Students To ...

Faculty congeniality is essential to good teaching. I was very lucky to work with people who all got along and genuinely liked each other. We did things together, like attending football games and showing up four hours early when big games were at hand. Yes, one year in rather inclement weather a group of us arrived at a sold-out game at 10 AM for a 2 PM start. We brought coffee, submarine sandwiches, and quarterly exams we had just given that week in class to correct as we sat in the damp stands, patiently waiting for the kickoff.

We were young and devoted. We enjoyed our jobs and we loved the kids. We had a ball and celebrated after a big victory with supper and fun. At another such occasion, we were celebrating at our favorite spot; the dance band was playing football songs, and the crowd included a group of parents whose children we had in school.

We were loud, singing well-known tunes as the band played Notre Dame's victory song as well as our own school's rah-rah songs. As the evening progressed, we were awarded with a round of drinks from the parents who spotted us and waved and encouraged our good time. I will never forget it. We appreciated being treated as normal people, even though we were their kids' teachers.

⬤▬▬▬▬▷

My first-year speech as president of the teachers' association included this closing:

"As I stand before you, I represent a product of this school system who was from a broken home, but who was lucky to have wonderful family behind him.

"I loved school and decided it would be great to get paid for it, so I became a teacher. My uncles were superintendents and principals, but I loved to work with kids directly, so I decided to teach.

"I started in my hometown, even though I said I'd never teach here. I have spent countless hours as a teacher, advisor, play director after school.

"I got married last year, and this year ran for president and won! I want to lead you to great things. Will you please join me and support me when I ask for it? Will you please feel free to call on me for anything, because I want to make this association the best in the state.

"I hope you will all use the pen you received this morning from NTA. Remember, they're in our association colors of black and blue! Have a wonderful school year, and I hope you all have the best and the brightest students you ever had in your lives! Thank you

⬤▬▬▬▬▷

During my second year as president of the association, I given five minutes to make my opening day remarks. Since we had a grievance pending, I seized the moment and gave the following satirical remarks.."

When I asked to be on the program this morning, I was told that I would have five minutes! Me do something in five minutes? Okay, you get lemons—you make lemonade! What could I say in that small amount of time? Being a history teacher, I turned, of course, to that great orator, Abraham Lincoln, who gave one of the greatest addresses in history in a short amount of time, so here goes—with all due apologies to our sixteenth president:

"One score and two days from now, our association will bring forth in this school system an arbitration conceived in liberty and dedicated to the proposition that all teachers are treated equal.

"Now we are engaged in a great grievance, testing whether our teacher or any teacher so conceived and so dedicated can long endure.

"We have met in a great school system of that grievance. We have come to make sure a teacher of that association who has put in twenty-eight years in this profession, and all of us, might live.

"It is altogether fitting and proper that we should do this. But, in a larger sense, we cannot grieve, we can not consecrate, we cannot hallow this association.

"The brave teachers, living and dead, who struggled here consecrated it far above our poor power to add or detract.

"The city will little note nor long remember what we say here, but it can never forget what we did here.

"It is for us, the current staff, to be dedicated here to the unfinished work which we who fought last year and have thus far so nobly advanced.

"It is rather for us here dedicated to the great task remaining before us—that for our grievance, we take increased devotion to that cause for which we give our last measure of devotion—that we highly resolve that this arbitration shall not be in vain, that this association's contract under us shall have a new birth of freedom.

"And that this association of the teachers, by the teachers, and for the teachers shall not perish from the earth!"

CHAPTER 7
There Will Be an Emergency Faculty Meeting at 2:15

Fast replies and quick comebacks sometimes help teachers in awkward situations. One such time, a colleague of mine was confronted by a student as to why he got a failing grade. When approaching my friend, the student said, "Why did I get an F?"

Rather than say *that's what you deserved or earned*, this teacher came right back and said, "Because there's nothing lower!"

—————

"Boys will be boys" was often heard when teenagers got out of control or did stupid, manly things that were totally uncalled for. One such time occurred in my teaching career. A group of boys had gotten into big trouble one weekend by entering a tomb in a local cemetery and rearranging corpses in comical situations. Unique but immature. Yet the town fathers thought it so irritating that names were never released or any action taken because of who was involved. I had nothing but repulsive thoughts when I heard that some cadavers were placed around a table as if playing cards with a real deck of fifty-two playing cards provided by this group. Teenage drinking took a big hit after this was whispered around town, and shortly after that, I voted to raise the drinking age back up to twenty-one.

I was thrown into a big teacher problem in my first year as president of the association. A good, respected teacher had applied for personal leave, which is a perk of the contract if used for legal reasons. This woman wanted to use the four days for a trip to England, to visit her son at Oxford University. This was to be during a week that used to be a school vacation, before our illustrious school committee changed things that year to one vacation in March, instead of the traditional February and April months.

She was denied, and we were forced to grieve it, since the school committee was going against past practice. She had gone by herself to see the superintendent, in hopes of rectifying the situation. Since we had no witness as to what happened other than this teacher, it came down to the super's word against our member's. As time went by, we did educate our staff not to see the administration by themselves if it was job-related. They hadn't been educated to do this by previous association presidents.

Despite many attempts not to arbitrate, we were forced to, due to the immobile school committee's closed minds. We followed the contract to the letter, and finally had to call other teachers as witnesses who had been granted to them to support our colleague. One teacher had gotten an okay to use the personal days for an Italian trip and skied, and one was okayed to visit and take part with her dog in the Westminster Dog Show in New York! But our colleague was denied an educational trip to a great university to see her son, who was one of twenty in the Untied States to attend Oxford on scholarship that year.

I met with the superintendent to try to strike a compromise before all this happened. Being new, she would have none of it. She said that if the system allowed this for this teacher, who knew how many more would ask for their personal days? I said that our teachers did not and would not take advantage of the situation, but that fell on deaf ears, too.

After weeks of waiting, the arbitrator ruled in our favor, and although too late to satisfy our member, precedent was set, and no one was denied again. Personal days are personal, but our teachers were still required to give a reason, and some still had to go visit the principal before they were granted permission for something that is in the contract and never abused by any of our teachers.

I learned a lot from this episode that would come in handy in later years as president of the teachers' association. Power is something administrators covet, and if there is any suggestion toward erosion, they go absolutely ballistic, even if it's common sense to give teachers what is rightfully theirs. Little do administrators realize that if they played ball with teachers, they could get so much more done. Unfortunately, they just don't get it. They never have and they never will, and I attribute that to power and control. Someone once said power corrupts and absolute power corrupts absolutely.

School buildings are sick and making those who inhabit them sick too. Newburyport was no exception, even though it was denied many times by the powers that be. An elementary school in our district had two women teachers die and another so sick she couldn't return to the school. I tried many times to have the buildings periodically inspected for allergies, since I developed them quite late in my career. After being tested and medicated, I asked my allergist for help. He gave me an address and phone number of the official to call in the State House in Boston. He conducted an exhaustive evaluation of the high school and one elementary school. If the high school didn't undergo extensive renovations in the first two years of the new millennium, I am sure the report would have been instrumental in closing the place. But we did undergo great renovations and expansion of our sixty-five-year-old building.

In order to do this successfully, we moved out and spent two years in the middle school building, sharing that place with half the staff and students. The rest of the middle school folk were housed in an available vacant school in a nearby town. However, one teacher who was a student in the middle school years ago developed a recurrence of her allergies when she returned to teach there. It certainly was amazing that this woman had allergies as a seventh grader, but once out of that place as a high school and college student, had nothing. When she returned to teach at the middle school, all her old allergies re-appeared!

What can be done? Massive testing and cleanup is essential in all schools across America. Industries would be shut down if companies made their employees experience what teachers and kids go through daily. Chalk dust, ventilators that are never cleaned, and carpet that is never cleaned or replaced in twenty years are a few things that must be dealt with in dealing with sick school buildings. This generation of children is so susceptible to asthma and allergies, one wonders if schools aren't contributing to their ill health.

CHAPTER 8
Please Do Not Allow Students to Stand When Finished

A fter teaching theatre arts for seventeen years of my thirty-seven-year career, I am firmly convinced that fine-arts education should be required of all students in high school.

Students are very creative, and yet we stifle this creativity in all of them by not demanding that at least three credits of their total requirement for a high school diploma be in the arts. Societies lacking in the arts are usually ones in which more crimes are happening, from robberies to mate abuse. William Bennett in the foreword to *Against Mediocrity: The Humanities in American High Schools* states:

"It is not the deep musings that we need in high school, not the intense scrutiny of profundities, but rather a basic group of the themes, ideas, and figures that have made our culture. These can be found in the Arts."

He continues, "A thousand hours a year of television viewing and other cultural suppressants have left a sensibility that is often deficient. Acquaintance with some of the best that has been known may provide a much-needed corrective." Fine arts is the answer.

Peter Greer states, "Do our history courses include intellectual, cultural and social history? Do they pay attention to the historical development and cultural significance of art and music?" The answer is obviously, NO. They don't. He goes on to state that "Education is an enterprise of intellect and spirit. We have forgotten our mission and are living like monks in a monastery. Our students leave our schools filled with career plans but baffled by or heedless of timely and timeless issues, good books, and a quality of their inner lives" that only the arts can provide. "What we can do to affect needed reform in the humanities in our school is clear. The only question is whether we have the nerve to do it!"

Finally, Harry S. Broundy states—and this is certainly true today—"in times of trouble we still turn to the humanities for guidance (literature, philosophy, theatre and music.)" Our students would welcome this requirement with open arms! They want creative courses that only the fine arts can give them. What are we waiting for?

For the first time in our country's history, the educational skills of one generation will not surpass, will not equal, will not even approach those of their parents. We have become a country with a fascination for the "merely contemporary." The humanities lie "shattered," Bennett states.

"It is difficult to define the humanities and it is bad education to apply a scientific method to the humanities since so many courses focused on affective goals rather than on content or cognition." Peter Greer makes this point in defending the arts for their solid educational base. However, he continues, "Humanities need the support of administrators. The possibilities are vast, limited only by the scope of one's imagination and the extent of one's energies."

The national commission of "A Nation at Risk" in 1984 urged disciplined study of the humanities as a guide both to better self-knowledge and to keener appreciation of the achievements of our culture and civilization. Peter Greer concludes, "Let us invite students into the humanities by consideration of great literature, seminal history, and the importance of ideas so in the spirit of Plato, they at least may know what they don't know! Schools must take the lead for the humanities to compete with other forces shaping students' minds and allegiances."

Special education (or SPED) has had tremendous effects on public education since its inception in the 1970s. Students with learning disabilities are helped by aides and alternative programs designed to give them high school diplomas they might otherwise not attain. Unfortunately, true SPED kids are being forced to share their problems with others who are more discipline cases.

SPED kids can have individual education plans or IEPs written for them that the classroom teachers must incorporate in their classes. Planning for the future it held each spring when IEPs are done and of which I attended until it became obvious that this took too much of my time besides my regular teaching duties. Once in a while, if I really felt I could be of help, I would go. This occurred a special needs student of mine, Jonathan, was having his IEP proposed for next year. I arrived and found his mother had been accompanied by an advocate from the state, who was demanding everything for Jon just like regular kids. I remember with great interest the poor kid sitting next to me, cringing when the advocate demanded a lab science for this boy, even though he barely passed physical science the previous year. Jon whispered to me that he could never pass a lab science, even with great tutoring. I nodded and told him under my breath to sit tight and we would change it later. Sure enough, as the next year came and Jon failed the lab science first quarter, we switched him to a current-event-related science for life type course, which he passed.

Under Massachusetts law, money must be provided in school budgets to provide education for SPED kids until age twenty-two. Students are encouraged to do what they can on a test, take the test in a learning lab in each school, where tutors will aid them, and not be afraid to cry out for help. Students cannot be isolated from their classmates, and must be mainstreamed—included in regular classroom settings. If they can't take notes, their tutor goes to class with them and does it for them.

Public schools should say no to such demands, but if they do, then they lose massive state aid and could be in court! Outside placements to schools that deal with extreme hardship cases are very expensive and can drain as much as $70,000 per student from a public school system.

<hr/>

Foreign students are leading the Americans around by the nose, and I say more power to them. In all my years of teaching, I have had some great kids from other countries either as exchange students or new arrivals to this land.

One was a delightful person originally from Thailand. She was here living with her closest relatives since her parents were killed in the Vietnam conflict years ago. This little girl was so good that I had to mark her twice with quarterly grades of A+. I never did that before or since in my entire thirty-seven-year career. The reasons were many, like smiley attitude daily, near-perfect attendance, intelligent questioning, always being on time, scoring straight A's on every quiz and test, and a great eagerness to learn, unlike her American counterparts who were so apathetic, it was almost catching among them.

Another girl was from Russia as an exchange student one year. Marina was a delight but older and ready for college upon her return to her native land. She was so outstanding that I awarded her the American History Medal at the school's annual awards assembly. My colleagues were aghast to think of a Russian getting recognized for American history! But she was the best, and that is what we were praising, I rationalized. I stuck to my guns and she received the medal!

Both these kids were fun to teach and appreciated the hard work of American teachers. Many times they told me I worked too hard and did too much for my students. They couldn't even comprehend why we tested students so much, like giving weekly quizzes. They said that if students failed, it was their fault, not the teacher's.

I remember once at a shopping mall when I ran into a former student who didn't recognize me after many years had passed and he had been out of school a while.

I recognized him as we got closer, I said,

"Hi, Tim, how you doing?"

He looked at me and replied, "Didn't you used to be Mr. Doyle?"

I said, "Yes, Tim, I still am!"

CHAPTER 9
My Dog Ate My Homework

At the end of each semester recently, I polled my classes in US Government to find out their reactions to a few things like:

What is the biggest problem in the world? First place—world hunger; second place—global warming; third place—(in no particular order) attitudes, energy, greed, inequality, pollution, caring people, health.

What should the US do? 1. Nothing. 2. Help others, take a strong stand, stop complaining, start small, prevention, pay closer attention, elect a caring president, not eat so much, watch terrorists, build more refineries, give money to health, watch and research, give food to suffering countries.

What can YOU do? 1. Nothing. 2. The same. 3. Make people more aware, give food to charities, become more active, feel terrible, join Greenpeace, donate, act equal, don't let it bother me, tell people, help people, be positive, complain more, be vocal, petition the government for action.

Who was the best president in your lifetime? 1. Clinton. 2. Reagan.

Who was the best president ever? 1. Franklin Roosevelt. 2. John F. Kennedy. 3. Dwight Eisenhower.

Who was the worst president ever? 1. Richard Nixon. 2. George W. Bush. 3. Lyndon Johnson.

What will bring you happiness? 1. A good education and career. 2. Meaningful job that aids people. 3. Good people and mate. 4. Success and love. 5. Friends and people. 6. Make the world a better place; good job. 7. Being healthy and active. 8. Simplicity and good family. 9. Nice car.

What will be your career in ten years? 1. Engineering and teaching. 2. Linguist, chiropractor, sports management, commercial artist, public relations, actress, psychologist.

What was the best thing you got out of high school? 1. Friendships. 2. A diploma. 3. Future good education. 4. Good essay-writing. 5. Half-baked M&M cookies!

The high school would be a better place if … 1. Better AP classes, more resources, more energetic teaching. 2. Better food, better discipline, start school later, more electives. 3. Eliminating certain groups and cliques, more diversity, interesting assemblies to add to the curriculum, open campus.

Responses from another class were unique just on the definition of happiness, and they are as follows:

Happiness is—

—a method of life that requires effort at times. You must create your own happiness.

—the right to have and due [do] whatever you want.

—when they legalize it—ha, ha, ha!

—everything going MY way.

—ignorance!

—skiing while eating a lobster roll!

—sleep!

—living the life in the Bahamas and being a millionaire.

—doing what you feel is necessary.

—having fun and enjoying what your [you're] doing.

—appreciating the small stuff.

—summer and hanging with friends.

—when I'm not here!

Another group answered the question:

"What will you be doing ten years from today?"

—living in California with a good job (something to do with entertainment, radio or film)

—network administrator

—counting stacks of money, sittin' poolside with a beautiful wife

—rich, gorgeous wife, really nice cars, and set for life

—I don't know!

—a rich housewife

—sittin' next to a pool, drinkin' beer, smoking a cigarette, listening to Sublime

—public relations graduate working for a large company, making great money, had one child, and work part time as a lobbyist for G.O.A.L.

—programming computers for six figures a year

—performing musically hopefully making a lot of money doing it

—living well, sleeping, working as little as possible, making a lot of $

—working at a hospital in ultrasound and living in Maine or Vermont

—performing with the Boston Pops or another well-known musical group

—hopefully I will have a good job, an awesome husband, and maybe a child or two

—an officer in the Marine Corps

—teaching history

—driving my many cars on my personal racetrack
—teaching dance in my own studio
—an early childhood teacher
—electrical engineering or law enforcement
—married with three children and own a bookstore and teach
  end grade
—on the streets— mooching off welfare!
—biotechnology— working to make cures for disease
—working on my PhD
—designing soundtracks for movies, living with my graphic
  designer/rock star boyfriend in a three-story apartment
—having a job that allows me to be creative artistically
—being a millionaire and philanthropist
—living in my own house with a sexy wife right next to a massive
  ski resort and being very financially set!

CHAPTER 10
No One in the Hall Without a Pass

Students need occasional guidance. I will never forget the time I heard a young girl in one of my shows crying backstage after a painting session one Saturday afternoon. While cleaning up and readying to go home, this fine young lady was sobbing out of control. I asked what was the matter and she said that due to a low grade in Spanish, she would probably have to drop out of the show.

No way was I going to let that happen, since we opened in two weeks, so I asked her to come with me. We sat down in the front row of the auditorium as the other kids finished the cleanup. She explained that she had flunked Spanish II and her parents were on her back to drop the show and study. I said that I would have other kids help tutor her, which we often did as a production team, just as long as she didn't drop out of the show at this late date. She was crying more now, and she told me how much she hated the teacher and how she wasn't as smart as her sister, who always got an A in Spanish.

I asked her if she went back for extra help, and how much she studied in an advanced course like second-year Spanish. I asked her what she got for a grade in Spanish I last year. She said nothing, so I repeated the question. She finally responded by saying that she never took Spanish. I told her to meet me on Monday morning in the guidance office and we would rectify her problem by getting her placed in Spanish I, which I did.

Teachers need an active association. For years, our association was extremely inactive, so I decided with negotiations coming up for new salaries again that I would take a workshop and volunteer my services to the negotiation team. I attended summer sessions on the topic and felt that I could contribute to the team. When I heard from the current president that my services would not be needed, I decided to challenge him for election as president. So I did and mounted a massive campaign to get fellow teachers committed to me when elections rolled around in the spring. I found out I would have to wait another year, due to a two-year term nobody knew anything about. I waited the year and ran for president.

It just so happened that negotiations were underway, and a planning session had to be interrupted to count the votes. I made sure that I was there and witnessed the proceedings myself. As I walked around the area, I could see that I was doing well, but I would have to wait until all votes were tallied. Once they were, I had won two to one over the incumbent and would become the new president in September.

I would never forget the elation of going to the state convention in Boston and telling everyone I knew that I had just been elected. I would have a big job ahead of me, but I did it and I was ready to give the teachers the leadership we had lacked for so long.

There has to be a fine line between students and teachers as to what can take place. Teachers must maintain a close relationship to do a good job, but not to the point of giving kids rides in their cars or bringing them into their homes. Male teachers have to be especially careful regarding anything that could possibly be taken as inappropriate. Teachers must not cross that line—period. If they do, then charges can be brought in court against the educator. Such an incident occurred during my very first year as president of the association.

Bruce was a veteran teacher of middle school students. He was a dynamic guy with lots of energy, and he engaged students in after-school activities that carried over into his home. After bike riding with boys in a school club, he would have them over to his house to watch videos and eat pizza. The time came when parents didn't like stories they heard about this type of activity, and they demanded that the school committee issue a policy forbidding it. The school committee and superintendent failed to take any action because they reasoned it would be impossible to enforce, and besides, teachers were adults and usually used good judgment. Besides, what they did in their private lives was no concern of the school system—as long as it didn't infringe on their job performance.

Very early one fall day, I was summoned to the superintendent's office and told that Bruce had been suspended with pay regarding inappropriate actions with young boys. There would be no more discussion about it, for the good of the school system. I contacted Bruce and told him that we would contact the state association to provide a lawyer for him, which we did. Two boys had come forward and were pressing charges against Bruce for indecent actions with children.

At the middle school, teachers work in teams, and team members were being summoned to voice their knowledge about this incident. Keep in mind that the philosophy of the middle school is to educate the total child, so various activities are encouraged and done by teachers to reach these kids beyond the normal classroom methods.

So serious was this affair that to inform the teachers, the administration from the superintendent's office made separate appearances at all five schools. They said that the law would be upheld and the schools would continue without interruption by the media. If we saw the press in our building, they were to be ignored and escorted out. Eventually the charges were made public, and the teachers handled it beautifully by carrying on and not letting it occupy their classes. Some the kids who had been victims of the allegations being brought to the forefront were now in high school.

In the meantime, the teachers' association president—namely me— was fielding questions from all over. What did the association intend to do if the charges were proven true? How could we defend somebody like that in education? What was happening to Bruce? What support were we going to offer? I called Bruce and told him that we were believers in and supporters of the Constitution of this country, and that no one was guilty until proven so. I explained that we would do everything to provide due process of the law, and I was with him until I couldn't be. He thanked me and appreciated my support and that of the association.

The case would ultimately take four years to resolve itself. Bruce was ordered to stay away from children under eighteen and to stay away from schools. The latter was pretty hard to do, since he lived just a block away. He continued to pay his union dues yearly, since he was still technically a teacher under suspension in the system. The gossip was ugly and vindictive. The stories were sad and depressing, especially if they ever turned out to be true. His teammates saw him as a fellow teacher and supported him as such. He was privileged to live the type of life he chose, but—being a teacher—raised other odds. Very few professions except teaching allow two generations (adults & kids) to meet daily in its pursued goals.

I told the teachers it didn't look good for Bruce, and the very next day was chastised by the administration for telling the truth. I was ordered to keep my mouth shut under threat of legal action. I told everybody not to discuss the situation with anybody but each other. In the meantime, the court wanted to ask teachers about the young man. We told the investigators that we were told that we couldn't discuss the case, under orders by the administration.

In a court judgment that ruled in our favor, a judge said that the administration couldn't put a gag order on teachers, since it would, in fact, hamper their own investigations. The police seized his computer and a video collection from his home. Boys had told of sexual encounters with Bruce and tapes he had made of them.

Before Christmas one year, I called Bruce, and he told me he thought he would be vindicated. One charge was already dropped, and he stood a good chance of winning the other, his lawyer said. He again thanked me for continued support as union president. Nothing happened for a long time, and the case was put off until further notice.

It seems some more boys had come forward and told of charges against Bruce. Trial was postponed until more work could be done.

CHAPTER 11
Disregard All Bells ...

About a year later, Bruce was freed on $10,000 bail on charges amounting to indecent assault and battery on a person under age fourteen by two former students. Police said that he sent the victim three computerized images of nude males. Another incident happened when a boy asked Bruce a few questions after class and Bruce said he would answer the boy's questions at his home. The boy got the address and rode his bike to Bruce's house, where the sexual assault allegedly occurred.

After the assault, the boy was threatened by Bruce, who said to the victim that if he told anyone, he would take his body to the ocean at low tide, and at high tide, he would be taken out to sea and never see his mother again. The boy's grades fell from A's and Bs to failure after the incident. Ultimately, the boy dropped out of school.

Bruce was relying on his lack of a prior record and adherence to the conditions of his bail. Pretrial publicity prompted others to come forward. Prosecutors said that Bruce took advantage of his position as a teacher to convince young boys to come to his home, and then manipulated them into keeping silent about their assaults.

Two months later, the court indicted Bruce on child rape charges, including one count of child rape, two counts of indecent assault and battery on a child under fourteen, and two counts of disseminating harmful matter to a minor. These charges occurred fourteen years apart, which makes one wonder about the administration allowing him to continue to teach and not taking any action, whether or not it could be enforced. Perhaps just having a policy on the books might have made him and others stop and think.

Police searched his home again and seized more than eighty videos, computer hardware and software, and various computer-generated images of nude young males. Magazines described by police as pornographic were also confiscated.

Through all this, the administration informed parents via letters that the investigation was ongoing, and all school personnel were required to neither discuss nor speculate on this matter.

Bruce felt sick to his stomach on these new charges, it was revealed in court. It brought back a lot of bad memories, and he felt terrible that it hadn't been reported sooner. He felt he could have prevented it.

It was revealed that Bruce and the boy began an Internet correspondence, which culminated in Bruce's invitation to his home, where the assault occurred. Supposedly, Bruce sent the boy pornographic pictures via the Internet but it was not specified when the transmission occurred.

Police and the public wondered if more victims would come forward. It was shocking to the school system and the community, where nothing like this had ever occurred before. Parents were especially in shock over the school administrators' lack of action over rumors and students' stories. The parents felt they had proof. They explained the situation and where it could lead. They didn't understand why school officials seemed to brush it aside.

School administration said that the difficulty was that different charges forced the staff to be inundated with questions by the press and the kids. It made it harder to stay focused. The best tactic was to move forward while maintaining a consistent schedule.

Full concern had to be for the personal and emotional safety of the children, a letter to parents stated. The situation was based on limited information. An attempt to explain rape to schoolchildren was made by the school's principal. Adults did not help students by trying to shelter them from information they ultimately heard on television. Kids didn't do well, regardless of their age, if you didn't tell them what they're hearing and frame it for them, school officials stated.

The principal compared the situation to an earthquake, with many aftershocks to follow. Officials wanted to normalize the conversation around this for the kids while taking it seriously! Students were urged to refuse to talk to the press if asked, and told to reply, "No, thank you" if asked to comment.

Group counseling was instituted for students by school officials. Counselors were restrained from discussing this directly with students, however. Kids were hearing two things—if you need to talk, they're here for you. But people cannot talk to you about specifics of the case, a bulletin read. If students did have direct testimony, they would be referred to the police.

The purpose was not to create a vehicle by which they were internally investigating a police matter. They were definitely not trying to do that!

CHAPTER 12
Pardon the Interruption ...

Bruce pleaded innocent to all charges. He said that the actual cause of this was "bad blood" between himself and a student. He was able to get some of the bail money he had posted earlier, since the bail was reduced somewhat. However, the boy involved said that Bruce had asked him to look up pornography on a computer, unzipped his pants, and committed a sexual act. The boy was told not to tell anyone, because Bruce could lose his job. Parents objected to visits by youths to Bruce's house, but denied any sexual activity.

Another boy said that as part of a sexual unit being taught in the science class conducted by Bruce, he had been invited to Bruce's home to answer some questions the boy had raised in class.

Finally, a year later than it was originally scheduled, the case was ready for court, with five more charges announced. In total, this was three years after being charged and four years after I first learned about it.

Everyone was stunned as Bruce admitted that he was guilty of child rape involving one count of indecent assault and battery and one count of dissemination of harmful material to a minor and five counts of possession of child pornography.

He was not sentenced immediately, but was ordered to call the probation department every day. A recommended sentence was nine to twelve years in state prison, with ten years' probation, with conditions including sex-offender counseling and no contact with children under sixteen years of age.

A sickening feeling gripped my stomach when I heard about this. I went to the men's room and threw up, and later could not discuss it with my fellow teachers. I had been a defender and legal counsel advocate as president of the teachers' association. As I learned that Bruce had forced the boy to perform oral sex on him, over the boy's objection, I frankly could not believe it.

Teaching is a fabulous profession, and to have one of my fellow teachers totally disregard the children was abominable to me. I felt so sorry for the boys who were now in high school and were some of my students. They were reliving a horrible incident in their lives all over again. Counselors outside of school had heard about it and pursued the allegation by having police get a search warrant to go into Bruce's place. Bruce faced commitment from one day to life in a state mental hospital if the state declared him sexually dangerous before he was released from prison. He could be placed on lifetime parole supervision and registered as a sex offender.

Nothing in my training as president—or in my life in general—prepared me for this incident. To this day, I still feel extremely sorry for Bruce. But let's face it: He is an adult and students are children. I wonder why the administration at all levels ignored this whole thing and refused to take harsher action, but as you will see in a later chapter, they do not see things like teachers do.

CHAPTER 13
Is This Going to Be on the Test?

Of all the plays I did and I all musicals we presented, there was nothing like the time that we ran out of black hairspray for the male lead who happened to be a blonde. What to do? I told the girls in charge, "I don't care how you do it, but do it; get him black-haired by curtain time." It was for the final Saturday night performance, and in the 1980's stores were closed late in the evening when we were getting ready to go on, so you couldn't exactly go out and buy more black hairspray. As we met for the pre-curtain pep talk, I noticed they had done it all right. They had taken black eye mascara and totally transformed the boy into the character I wanted. He played a great Sergeant Trotter in "The Mousetrap" by Agatha Christie to perfection!

Newburyport like other schools is a football town. This was true for a great deal of my career, and is still true today, but certainly not to the extent it used to be. We had football rallies every Friday when I first started teaching. Nothing unusual, you may say. True enough, but as the team was winning for the first time in many a year, we also had them every Monday after they won! Football really was the only game in town then, whereas we have soccer and cross country now, and it looks like lacrosse in the near future.

Nothing can compare with the thrill of when a student actually comprehends what you are teaching. Even better is when you meet your former students outside of school and they remember what they learned from you. Such is the case in two incidents I never forgot. One was when a young waitress in a restaurant stopped and said that she voted today—which just happened to be Election Day—because of me. She explained that she knew it was time to vote because I made her and other students remember the following little ditty:

"We vote for president on the first Tuesday in November after the first Monday every four years if it's divisible by four evenly."

The day of this encounter was Election Day for President Clinton, although she neglected to say who she had voted for!

Another time was when a student saw me in a store in the local downtown and said she saw Oliver North in town and immediately thought of me and all we had covered in her class regarding the Contra Affair of the Reagan years. She thought he looked shifty.

Teenage pranks around April 1 were quite common and unique during my career as a high school teacher. The imagination used by teenagers to come with something different each each always blew me away. First of all, you have to distinguish that a prank is funny and not financially costly. Vandalism, on the other hand, is not cute and cuts into strapped financial school budgets to repair.

The very best prank was one April 1 eve, when senior boys got the keys to the alarm system and shut the alarms off. For endless hours, they took every single classroom tablet armchair desk out of every second- and third-floor classroom and brought them to the school library, where they stacked them floor to ceiling. Once we arrived for school on April 1, no one had a desk in his classroom. Over the PA, the principal made the announcement that everyone should report to the library to retrieve two desks each and bring them back to the classrooms immediately!

This was funny and enjoyed by all. The administration had many suspects, but never really found out how they got into the school to shut the alarms off. Another time, every chair vanished from the cafeteria. We were in the building for a school council meeting, and once the custodian on duty informed the principal, we went searching around the whole school. It looked like a perfect caper because no one could find the missing chairs. One by one, we reported to the auditorium and sat down, quite pooped from running around the school in our search. Finally, when we were relaying tales to one another of our unsuccessful attempts to find said chairs, I looked toward the stage. The rear curtain to the stage was drawn shut, which was unusual, since I always kept it open. I summoned another teacher to go up and pull the curtain open. As she did, there they were—more than 300 chairs, stacked neatly as far as the eye could see.

Not too funny or cute was one escapade that got carried too far. One year, the seniors had a load of cow manure dumped near the front door. They ordered white mice and birds from a science catalog and stuffed them in the senior lockers. When the lockers were open in the morning on April 1, girls screamed and slammed the lockers, cutting off tails and heads of scrambling mice.

The ASPCA was called, and charges were brought against two or three senior boys, because they had ordered lovebirds and separated them in this caper. These birds can die if separated. Also, much graffiti was painted on the school with spray cans and had to be sandblasted off. Seniors were made to pay for this damage from their class treasury, and this left less money for their senior celebration later on in June.

Not too bright a group ordered 200 crickets to be stuffed in lockers for a recent April 1 prank, but it backfired, as crickets only come out and chirp at night when nobody was in school!

In the northeastern part of the United States, especially New England, the school calendar is built around two breaks after Christmas. One week's vacation is allowed in February and another in April. The rationale is that as the year rolls on, sickness creeps into the buildings, as flu is rampant. The daylight hours are longer in the northeast and usually winters are harsh. All this traditionally makes the two school vacations a welcome relief for all teachers and students involved. For thirty-five years of my thirty-seven-year career, this was the case, except for a two-year period when a calendar was adopted that contained a March vacation only!

I was not president of the teachers' association yet when it as passed, but once I got in office, people asked me what we were going to do about the apparent fait accompli. I wanted the two breaks as much as anybody else, and decided to approach the superintendent about changing it after one year passed.

We had already had the personal day grievance over the week's visit to London that was denied one of our members, since she had scheduled it during a regular February vacation, not knowing the school committee would pull this boner of a March break. We polled our members, and people didn't enjoy the extended period of time from Christmas to March with no break. And even worse was the March-to-June time with no break as the weather heated up.

What got thrown in my face was that New England was out of step with the rest of the country, because nowhere else in the USA did schools have two weeks off after Christmas. If we went with the March break, we could anticipate an earlier release in June—barring no snow days—and that would be a plus. Our expanded state curriculum required more time on task, so one break would be much better. And with so many youngsters in day care, what could working mothers of elementary school-age children possibly do with their kids during these two weeks?

I explained that we made out just fine for years with the traditional calendar, and asked what great educational research they could show me that this would help our students. Parents already informed the school committee that they had vacation plans for years to Disneyland, and they certainly weren't going to lose money by not going in February or April.

Teachers were expected not to schedule vacations in February or April by using their personal days. If they did, they would be denied, as was our teacher who was visiting her son at Oxford. As association president, I told people we could do nothing about the first year, but we could try to change the school committee's collective minds for extending it for two years.

So that was our case as we mounted our plan. Kids were wonderful, and mounted plans of their own. Letters poured into the local paper from parents who didn't like the scheme one single bit. I personally met individually with most of the seven school committee members. Most were very receptive and sympathetic to my cause. A couple were not in the least interested in listening to me, since their minds were incapable of changing.

We flooded the room on the date when the new calendar was to be passed out for the next school year. Students and teachers argued that the new schedule would affect students who take part in music and drama festivals, sports and college visits, and teachers who take graduate courses during the normal vacation breaks. They made the case for the need to battle stress from recent midyear exams and winter illnesses.

High school students presented a petition with 85 percent of the school signing it, opposing the change. I told the group that lots of problems had arisen, and low morale was running rampant among teachers. A parent told the school committee that in his research, many Midwestern states had a single week of vacation, and it was horrible. They were going back to the two vacation times the next school year.

An extremely weak argument from the school committee was that they had entered the scheme with two neighboring districts, and if they voted to change, they would be going back on the pledge to the two others. Many reminded them that they were elected to serve our interests, and to hell with neighboring towns.

A very outspoken school committee member—who obviously had never taught a day of school—said that students go from September 1 to Christmas—fifteen weeks—and don't die! Other members tried to blame the weak professional conditions board made up to teachers and school committee members for not raising the issue first. Misleading and confused statements tried to place the blame on association leadership, like we were for it when the contract was negotiated, and now we were trying to change our position. Of course, this neglects the fact that association leadership itself changed when I assumed the presidency!

Students felt added frustration because they were being given the runaround when they approached the mayor and school committee members. School principals were no help to the students either. The mayor in particular was just spectacular. When students said that one March vacation caused stress for kids, and that had to be given attention, the mayor fired back that kids didn't know stress until they reached her age and they didn't have a vacation all year.

One school committee member offered this encouraging idea, saying "What information did they have that one vacation was better than two?"

Also, with the state adding the standardized tests to graduation requirements, teachers wouldn't have kids properly rested if March was the only vacation instead of February and April, like other schools in the commonwealth of Massachusetts. A fellow teacher asked what was wrong with a break from the routine—it serves our mission as a school better and two vacations do this better than one.

After two and a half hours, the vote was taken, and when it was tied three to three, it was up to the mayor to break the tie, and she voted no. A very audible gasp was heard throughout the room.

We had lost by one vote, and we were stuck with the March vacation for another miserable year.

On opening day the next September, the mayor came up to me and said that she didn't understand the vote at the meeting, and wished then that she had voted yes.

I was absolutely stunned and just stood there speechless!

When the calendar was up for discussion again the next year, we didn't have to fight it to change back, because we made our point. Every school committeeperson I spoke to realized that we weren't giving up. They knew there were more important educational items to talk about, so they would not extend the March vacation beyond the two-year commitment.

We won, but suffered immensely for two wicked years under what was known—not very fondly, I might add—as "March Madness"!

CHAPTER 14
My Printer Doesn't Work

WHAT'S THE BEST THING YOU GOT
OUT OF HIGH SCHOOL?
Asked of seniors about to graduate ...

—The awareness to not send my nephew here.
—How much you got out of this institution is what you put into it.
—I've got some "stones" about the faculty in this school— the teachers rock but the administration are fascists— power-hungry fascists!
—maturity and social understanding
—learning from the acting teacher
—A Mr. Doyle education!
—friends
—party life and Doyle's class
—getting involved and working to get ahead
—not to take my life too seriously and a love for biology
—my friends and an appreciation for sleep and free time
—to understand who I really am

—enough knowledge of politics to know that G.W. Bush is an idiot
—to realize that sometimes it's better just to keep your mouth shut than state your own feelings and don't get caught up in gossip
—how to properly write an essay
—the more people you know, the more favors you can have done for you under the table.
—having Mr. Doyle
—the little life lessons you learn from making mistakes
—a diploma
—tolerance for beer
—graduation
—um?? I really don't know
—an education— ha ha
—how to fit a lot of students into a small building
—a girlfriend
—improving of my speaking skills
—learning how to BS so well I passed with flying colors!
—too many things happen during high school to put just one first!

CHAPTER 15
Please Pick Up the Paper on the Floor ...

An exceptional October morning greeted me as I went to fetch the newspaper. A "V" of geese flew overhead, honking their familiar yet uncommon sound. It is one of the very few pleasures we can rely on, getting up so early, and it's nice to know that it is a yearly occurrence. As I looked up through the brilliantly colorful red and yellow trees to find the flight, I discovered a patch of blue sky. Sure enough, there they were, swiftly flying south for the winter, hopefully avoiding hunters' deadly blasts along their way. It was a wondrous sight.

I skimmed the Boston daily, as I always did before my drive along the river to my school. Later, as I drove eastward, the sun was rapidly burning off a scant fog that was absent inland. And once over the two familiar bridges many of us crossed on our way to work, it had dissipated.

Once on the main street, I proceeded quickly until I approached an elementary school. There wasn't too much traffic yet; not many kids or morning joggers either. The street was relatively empty, except for two third- or fourth-grade boys who were carrying musical-instrument cases and attempting to cross the street. I looked for the crossing guard with her portable stop sign, but she wasn't there yet.

Undaunted, the lead child, with his hand up to slow traffic in both directions, moved rapidly across as the other followed in tow. It was great! Safely across, the two scampered up the school's driveway, grinning ear to ear.

In a short span of time, I had witnessed two enjoyable seasonal events this October daybreak. This satisfaction was something that renewed itself daily, weekly, and seasonally. It was one of the perks of being a New England teacher.

Funny tests answers continued throughout my career but this one is unforgettable.

Asked to Identify the Prime Minister of Great Britain who was trying to appease Adolf Hitler by having him sign the Munich Pact in 1938.

One student wrote Wilt Chamberlain who was the powerhouse center for the Philadelphia Seventy-Sixers and very much in the news during the time we were learning about World War II in the late 1960s! The correct answer was Neville Chamberlain.

CHAPTER 16

If You Want Your Midyear Exams Typed, They Must Be in before Christmas …

"Have a nice weekend. I have to see you first thing Monday morning." So said the principal as she bid me adieu the first Friday of the new school year.

All weekend I wondered what I had done to merit that message. Did I offend her? Was some student complaining about my class already? What could it be?

It turned out to be the biggest episode of public education I ever was privy to witness in my entire thirty-seven-year career. When it was over, three school leaders changed their jobs, and a teacher would be absolutely devastated for life. It would last for one month and one day before it was finally resolved. It would have devastating effects on many lives in the teaching profession for a long, long time.

Once Monday came, I arrived at school and made my way into the principal's office, passing two substitute teachers sitting in the outer office. The principal told me that the boys' soccer coach was going to be placed on indefinite paid administrative leave, due to an incident on a team bus following a pre-season scrimmage. Hazing was the topic she stated to me that they were looking into, and the administration had verbal evidence from kids that he had done nothing to stop it.

I was told to come back as soon as possible, and she would send for the coach and his wife—who was also a teacher in the high school—to take him home once she explained to him what was up. I couldn't believe my ears, but I knew that this wasn't going to be a typical Monday by any stretch of the imagination. I would get my classes covered so that I could contact Massachusetts Teachers Association legal services in Boston as president.

After about a half hour had passed, I sat in the principal's office with the dean of student support, dean of student affairs, and the soccer coach. The principal read the charge and he sat there, absolutely thunderstruck. I am accused of what? he must have thought. My inner strength rallied, and I swung into action, preparing to defend a colleague, an honorable man, and a true friend for close to thirty-five years. I phoned the state association. I phoned the regional office. I started the ball rolling to obtain aid for this man.

Any teacher could be sitting here, I thought as I began my lonely crusade. After explaining what I could do for him, I was alone and on the phone. I was too dazed to realize what came next; I just did it. My contact at the regional office was the first to reply. The lawyer in Boston was wonderful as I talked to her. The morning was flying by, and I was doing everything I could remember from my presidential training and in my caring for this fellow teacher. In spite of everything I knew, he was a victim, and I knew we would get him due process. I taught, but now I was actually doing it!

He was home and out of the building. My thoughts were with him, so I phoned him. I told him not to talk to anyone unless he had legal representation. I ate a quick lunch and conducted business on the phone. I called Boston again and obtained an official form via fax that would get him legal representation. I had to request this for my friend. I did it and it was received! Our MTA consultant called him at home and reassured him of his rights and of himself. It was now school dismissal time, and I still wasn't through. I had to see the administration again. They were at best concerned.

I was on my way home and my cell phone rang. Our consultant had reported that legal services were finalized, if and when our teacher would need them! I ordered a basket of fruit at a store for him and sent it from all of us. I got home and he called me, profusely thanking me for what I had done all day for him. I couldn't believe it. I ate supper and called him, as I told him I would each day. He was very appreciative and still stunned. Each day of the week, I had been encouraged by the help of our tremendous state association. Each day of the week, I listened to rumors and stories, and I was sickened by the low morale all this had caused. I didn't stop until my colleague was back teaching and coaching and vindicated. He had done nothing wrong. I was totally drained. Could anyone imagine how he felt?

CHAPTER 17

You Must Leave Emergency Plans if You Are Out Unexpectedly

How did this come to be? It seems that younger team members were talking about the annual rite of passage of receiving wedgies from older members on the back of the bus and a parent overheard them. Instead of going to the coach, the superintendent was informed. She consulted the system's lawyer from Boston, and the coach was suspended—boom! It would have made better sense to have the administration call in the man and warn that if it happened again, he would be suspended or gone as a coach. Why was he suspended as a teacher? This so-called incident didn't occur in his classroom.

Let's meet the cast of characters "in charge." First we have a new female superintendent, totally inexperienced in her new job. Second we have a female principal who didn't understand the male passage thing at all. And finally we have a new athletic director who should have defended a coach of his and taken action—instead of me, the union president—but he was on non-professional status.

When I reached home that first night, my message machine was loaded and the phone just never stopped ringing. I had to go through the whole thing so many times, I finally asked the callers what they knew and what they wanted to find out from me.

Hazing is against the law and school rules. Public schools do not condone such behavior. Organizers and participants can be fined up to $3,000 and sentenced to a house of correction for up to one year under state law, if found guilty. Those who witness hazing can be fined up to $1,000 if they fail to report the incident. Secondary and post-secondary schools are required to circulate copies of state anti-hazing laws to all their students as well as affiliated student teams and organizations annually.

If my friend and co-worker was suspended for seven days, what about the kids who did this thing? It seems after administrative investigation that they only got one day of in-school suspension! Justice is not equal. Fairness and the ability to face your accusers was what I was after through all this, because quite obviously, this was not done.

As Association president I immediately informed our teacher members what had happened and issued a statement as follows:

"The Newburyport Teachers Association is both stunned and disappointed in the lack of discretion accorded this teacher by the high school and central office. The fact that they have been so secretive to him while so forthcoming to be quoted in the local paper highlights their insensitivity to a man with a stellar reputation in this community for thirtfive years."

The superintendent added fuel to the fire by stating in the local press that the incident had involved physical touching, but refused to describe what the suspended students allegedly did in detail. Our member teacher was suspended for poor management of the bus and supervision students received.

By the end of September, the teachers' association released a memo to the administrators, as defense of the veteran teacher increased. In it, we threatened to advise teachers to suspend their student supervisory functions and extracurricular activities if the administration did not provide (a) written clarification of procedures governing the supervision of students outside of school hours and (b) the creation of a mutually acceptable and clearly articulated investigatory protocol.

Our group demanded visual support of our fellow teacher, and we ordered buttons stating "Newburyport United Teaching Staff" in school colors that we wore everywhere; they became very hot items!

At the beginning of October, the MTA retained the attorney I had wanted for this and released a scathing letter to the administration's attorney stating:

"Since it is conceded that our teacher did not know of the incident, was totally unaware of the incident, and did not condone the incident, we find the concept of this teacher is going to be suspended and disciplined for something he did not know was happening to be, quite frankly, absurd!

"If we do have to grieve and arbitrate this matter, we will grieve it thoroughly and aggressively ... This is absolutely nonsensical issue and it is an utterly foolish case, grossly mishandled by the school department."

CHAPTER 18
Stay Tuned, It's Not Over—Yet!

The personal toll this whole thing was taking on everybody was absolutely unbelievable. Lack of any good leadership by the school administration was creating stress and tension for everybody. While it was obvious that they never expected the united support we mustered for our accused teacher/coach, we never expected such cold reactions to everything we tried to resolve the case.

The reaction to the whole situation went far beyond legalities and beyond the Newburyport teachers. While doing their best to dispel the problem, the administration—in a moment of really great intent—decided to meet with the students and set the record straight. Each class—senior through freshman—would be called to the auditorium and hear the superintendent and principal and then answer questions. Having seniors in class, I went to the auditorium during their time. Once I walked in, I knew instantly that this was going to be a "horror show." You have two rather reserved women trying to throw cold water on the affair, and instead added volatile gasoline!

The kids had threatened the day before to stage a sit-in out under a tree on school grounds, in order to support their teacher who was suspended. This alone should have signaled the administration about the high regard the kids had for our teacher. The protest was to be peaceful and short, and then the kids planned to re-enter the building and go on with the day.

As the auditorium meeting progressed, the kids were getting louder and more rambunctious because the women were not answering their questions. They were clearly avoiding the issues and could not give the kids any hope for our teacher's return. Rudeness on the kids' part bothered me, but the ineptness of the superintendent and principal bugged me more! It was increasingly obvious that neither had been in front of kids for quite some time, and they didn't know that they were digging themselves deeper and deeper as time went on.

Finally I could hear whispers of "let's walk out" or "let's get out of here" emanating from all over the audience. Then it just erupted and out the seniors went. As they passed the classrooms, they entered each one and asked the kids to follow. It was just like the Pied Piper of Hamelin. Everyone left the school orderly and finally were told to go home. All they were asking was the coach's reinstatement as soccer coach, an apology to him from the superintendent for excessive punishment, and guarantees that this would not happen again to another teacher.

As a faculty, we thought it would not be a big protest—until the auditorium meetings. We thought we had told the kids to be very careful that anything like a big disruption of the school could hurt the coach far more than help in the long run. Many of the students listened to us, and we estimated that ten to twenty kids would walk out regardless. As it turned out, the whole school evacuated!

The whole situation took on a life of its own in the month and a day of its existence, and got its own name. While I was paying the bill days later for the fruit basket I sent the first day, the clerk at the store said, "Is this for the 'Wedgiegate' incident?" I chuckled and repeated it to others as I was dealing with the situation. It stuck, and "Wedgiegate" it was and still is when we recall the whole thing.

Two days later, I issued with the principal a joint press release stating that the coach would be reinstated as coach, that the administration acknowledged that he neither knew about nor condoned the "wedgie" incident, and that the administration's concerns about supervision had been addressed in a mutually satisfactory manner.

Sometime through all this, a fellow history teacher gave me the following quote by Reverend Martin Niemoller from 1945:

"First they came for the communists, but I did not speak up because I wasn't a communist. Then they came for the Jews, but I didn't speak up because I wasn't a Jew. Then they came for the Catholics, but I didn't speak up because I was a Protestant. Then they came for me, and by that time, there was no one left to speak for me."

This pretty much summed up the feelings of all the teachers. We didn't deny that what happened on the bus happened. What we were very, very upset about was the fact that it could be any one of us on the line tomorrow if our teacher/coach didn't get due process. And the way he was taken out of the classroom by the administration that very first day was comparable to the worst that happened in Germany in World War II was done in front of his students, who never forgot this treatment and solidified their support for him.

I talked to my friend—our teacher/coach—many times over this thing. I asked him where he was on the bus and he said, as usual, he sat up front and watched the road. I asked him about his assistant—where was he? It seems the administration had hired one but didn't have confidence to have him on the bus to help. So what we had was one coach supervising more than forty students, when the normal load on a field trip ideally is one teacher to every ten students. And just where was the athletic director in all of this? I often wondered and still do, why he wasn't working with this coach on making sure correct personnel were assigned to the trips out of town.

If something like this was happening, why weren't the kids loud and voiceterous? Because they didn't want the coach to know they were giving "wedgies" to team members in the back of the bus!

I continued to receive phone calls and support from everybody. We were amazed at the letters to the editor that poured in from literally everywhere. They were written from neighboring towns and states, as well as one from Egypt! You'd think we orchestrated this, but we didn't. The teacher/coach was well respected and well loved by all, and the administration had picked on the wrong person to make an example of, if that was their mission. I sincerely doubted it then, and am still not convinced of it. I know they fumbled the ball from the get-go and didn't know how to save face.

One phone call I will never forget was from a lawyer friend who was representing an accused student. This lawyer was an ex-student of mine, and his family were friends of my family. He called me and just exclaimed how stupid this whole thing was, and related how inept the administration was handling it. He said that he met with the superintendent and was taken aback when he offered to talk common sense about the affair. The superintendent fired back that they weren't there to talk common sense! They were there to deal with an issue of student safety and that was it. Unbelievable.

I offered, in another phone call, to try to solve this thing to everyone's satisfaction—or so I thought—by dispensing with lawyers and sitting down in my home on a weekend with the accused and the accusers. I waited for a phone call back, but nothing ever came of it from anyone on the school committee or administration.

I was teaching full time and carrying on with my daily lesson planning. I was handling phone calls on my cell phone, since I couldn't rely on the school to relay messages fast enough. One day in particular, I recall that I requested from the school secretaries that any phone calls be put right through to my classroom, especially if the Boston lawyer was calling. At the end of the day, I went to my mailbox and discovered three phone message slips from the Boston attorney! I was too exhausted to scream at anybody, and just walked out to my car and drove home. It was after this that the association purchased a cell phone for me.

Still not getting anywhere regarding an apology from the administration, we decided to form an ad hoc committee and have our members attend the next school committee en masse. The ad hoc committee was a great aid to me, because I couldn't answer all the questions coming in, and everyone was eager to do something to help out. We met with our Massachusetts Teacher Association uniserv director one night and he cautioned us. He said that we should fully understand that actions we were taking like this could lead to people losing their jobs. To a man, each teacher there didn't care; it was the principle of the thing that bothered them the most. If an accusation like this could happen to a highly respected thirty-five-year veteran, it could happen to anyone. People demanded a public apology and were adamant about it. I knew this would not be easy, and events to come would prove me right.

One morning, I was called to the principal's office and told that we were to meet and come to a conclusion on this. She was being pressured to end it, and we were getting sick and tired of it too. The major people involved were summoned, and in we walked. I was there with my vice president of the association, the teacher/coach, the principal, dean of students, and dean of student affairs. For the next hour or so, we openly talked about the charges and what to do.

At one point, I knew we were not getting anywhere. The teacher and the dean were raising their voices and shouting at one another. You did this. I did not. You should have known. I did what I always did. On and on it went. I had given up note-taking and was very concerned that if this whole thing ever got out of hand, could any of us in the room restrain these two from physically hurting each other? The dean was a young man and the teacher/coach was a big man. I knew I could never come between them if they hit each other, and as I looked around, I thought no one else could either.

Somewhere in my presidential training and human smarts, I called a halt to the whole meeting and asked for a break. I knew that I had to get the players apart and out of the room. I told the principal that I was going into the next office and writing down three things to solve this whole mess. When I was through, we would come back and see if the administration would accept them. We ended the meeting. I asked my vice president to take the teacher/coach out of the building and drive around for another forty-five minutes to an hour with him after we discussed possible reconciliation objectives.

On a piece of scrap paper I found in the office, I wrote the following: One—the teacher be reinstated as a coach and teacher immediately. Two—no written accusations be placed in his folder. And three—an apology be issued to him by all involved. We thought these were the crux of the issue and what we wanted. The two left and I entered the principal's office. She was agreeable to the first two, but hedged on the last. We got two out of three, and once our individual lawyers saw them, we would meet and sign a joint statement.

I called our Boston attorney and called our teacher/coach, who was now home. They thought it looked okay, but were still skeptical. I was very tired and very hopeful at the same time.

I was elated when I arrived home that we had gotten this far, and went out to eat with my wife to celebrate. We arrived home and checked our messages. The teacher/coach and his wife had called, saying that they didn't like the fact that nothing was in the agreement about him not knowing what had happened on the bus, and that he was still being accused of allowing it, actually. I was devastated. I thought this whole thing could be back to square one again if they got too picky. I told them would call the principal at home, even though it was 10:30 at night, and get back to them, which I did.

The principal and I had a great talk. We both knew that we were on the edge of solving this, but if things were nitpicked, it could explode. She thought we could include language about their concerns, but doubted

70

we could agree about the apology part. I thanked her and told her I would continue this in the morning at school. I was still teaching—or attempting to—and I was very concerned that this should end.

Anyway, we turned up in the principal's office the next day and signed the paper with the addition that the teacher/coach wanted. We did not get the apology part, but would work on that later and more publicly. Our lawyer called and said that we had done well! He thought it was fine, and told us to have the teacher sign the agreement. Word spread like wildfire over this latest news. We had great support, but people still wanted the apology.

So we agreed that we would have a delegation attend the next school committee meeting in a week and demand an apology. We organized our members and alerted parents to attend. The kids wanted in and were going to be there too. We had to be very careful. I told everybody not to use the kids as pawns or talk about the situation in class when we should be teaching.

The meeting was announced, and boy, did we turn out! We had agreed that I would read a prepared statement, and just one other teacher would speak, so as not to push the school committee the wrong way. While waiting for people to arrive, we assembled in the school cafeteria and agreed to march in together as a sign of solidarity. Janitors were bringing in extra chairs when word leaked out that there were so many teachers in the cafeteria!

I did read my remarks and almost broke down due to the pressure and stress of the past four weeks. I apologized to my classes for having to devote so much time to this issue. I wanted my friend to be reinstated—period. I wanted everything I would want for myself if I were the one under the gun. The long, loud applause boosted my self-confidence and I sat down waiting for others to talk or the school committee to actually apologize. Wishful thinking, as it turned out. Others did talk, but they didn't sway the school committee to do anything. The first public comment was over. We drifted in and out of the room and planned our next strategy when public comment session number two appeared on the agenda.

It was really a work of art. Parents rose to our defense and said that the school committee should be ashamed at what they had put this teacher though. Then two lawyers rose and echoed a similar plea. An old school committee attorney spoke on our behalf and said that he hadn't done that in all the years he negotiated for the group, but this was an outrage. The applause was deafening, as one by one, students, teachers, parents, and friends rose to address the situation. Still, right to the very end, we had no apology.

The next day, rumors were rampant. We saw and heard about school committee members and administration coming and going from the principal's office. No one knew what was up, but at the end of the day, we were summoned to the school library, where the principal read an apologetic letter to the teacher/coach and his wife. It would not be until the next day that the story appeared in the local press, along with the superintendent's quasi-apology.

I was quoted as saying, "I think the apology is okay. It was very frustrating from all our viewpoints. From this side of the table, it took so long. I think last night's meeting had a tremendous effect. I just don't know why it took all that for them to do the right thing. I'll probably never know. It will take a long, long time to repair relationships. I think the lesson for both sides is number one, fairness and don't jump to snap decisions. Yes, the law is the law, but you also have to have human side to the law. In this situation, I saw no use of common sense, and that's truly unfortunate."

Our next move was to have a policy instituted to protect teachers. We wanted clear procedures and protocols but never saw anything concrete. We wanted this to be a key part of the next contractual negotiations. As I said at the time, "We've heard things are in the works, but I have to see things before I believe it."

If nothing else, this whole affair cemented the faculty and provided a wonderful friendship to materialize and grow between the people involved. My wife and I became close friends with the teacher/coach and his wife, and in another year's time, we retired together from great, long careers in education.

Three people changed their jobs for one reason or another. The principal retired at the end of the school year. The superintendent of schools asked for her contract not to be extended for another year. The mayor was defeated in her re-election bid the following November.

More amazing was the fact that the teacher/coach was never asked by the administration to explain his side of the story and has never been asked to this very day.

CHAPTER 19
Every Day in Every Way, People Are Getting Better and Better

Students revealed a lot to me in theatre arts. I recall one sincere boy who got the school nurse to excuse him from taking a shower after gym class. I couldn't believe it. I told him that he should suck it up and be a man and take the shower. "For God's sake," I said, "you're not going to get raped if you drop the soap!" The gym teacher was right there supervising, but the kid never took a shower. I often wondered what it was like in the next class he went to after gym.

Another time I was asked by a shy female student if she could have two history books—one to leave in school and another to leave at home, due to her medical condition. I later learned that she was anorexic, and school officials told her to make this request to all her teachers. I provided her with the two books and I thought that was the end of it.

One Friday night at a football game, I spotted her on the sidelines as a cheerleader, doing flips and jumps. I really couldn't believe my eyes!

If she was too weak to carry home a history book, where did she get the energy to be a cheerleader? On Monday morning, I went directly to the guidance office and asked what was up. I was told later that I was mistaken, and the cheering coach said it wasn't this particular girl at all. Baloney—my eyes never failed me, but my feet started to make their way much quicker toward retirement with this type of protecting students.

I used to be a real stickler for having history books brought to class by the students daily, but as the years went by, that changed too. It particularly came home to roost one day when I asked a boy where his book was when he asked to borrow one. He said that he couldn't remember, and that it could be in his mother's boyfriend's car, but they broke up Sunday night. I told him to go into the closet in the back of my room and get another for the class. Kids today have to deal with so much; I was grateful just to have him in class!

Not every student one meets is nice and ready to learn. Once, a student of mine didn't care for my class at all. She told me in no uncertain terms that she liked last year's history teacher much better than me. I really didn't care some days, so I just shot back to her that I just taught with everything I had and if she didn't learn anything, then that was her fault. After that, she never said a thing and we got along with a measured distance between us!

While teaching Contemporary Affairs, a senior elective, very often I would ask the class what topics they wanted to study. The list on the blackboard included abortion, nuclear power, capital punishment, terrorism, and so on—your usual listing for a class like this. The topics began to grow, and when one student yelled out euthenasia, one boy down back said, "I don't want to study that. What's wrong with youth in America!"

My wife was very heavily involved in local, state, and national teacher associations. On the night of the 2000 New Hampshire primary, we were in Manchester to await the victory of Al Gore over Bill Bradley. We arrived early and stood in the front row of the audience. It was absolutely packed and noisy. The excitement increased when we learned that John McCain had beaten George W. Bush. We then learned that Al had won and would be making an appearance before us very shortly. Sure enough, the music swelled and the crowd cheered loudly as he and Tipper made their way on stage. She introduced him and he gave a marvelous victory speech. After that was done, they both went in different directions to shake hands with the crowd. I could see them both as I turned my head side to side. They were getting closer and finally arrived near us. He shook my hand, I offered my congratulations, and he went on. She also shook my hand when she got to me, then suddenly spotted someone she knew behind me and leaned over to shake that person's hand. Apparently, this individual was further back, and as she leaned, I grabbed her with both my arms and held her up so she could greet this old buddy. Eventually she ended her greeting and regained her stability and moved on. I looked at my wife and said, "My God, I just held Tipper Gore in my arms!" I didn't come down from that for days and weeks afterward!

I remember once when I was proctoring a midyear exam. After I passed out the test, a student looked it over and yelled out, "Shit!" I immediately replied, "You do and you'll clean it up." Everyone laughed and the tension was broken. The exam commenced, and that was it.

What good would it have done to kick the kid out and make a big deal out of what a great majority of the others were probably thinking also?

I was on my way out of the school one day, when the head of the English department was passing by me, pushing a cartload of paperback books to distribute to her classes. I noticed stacks of the classic Silas Marner as she and I exchanged pleasantries. "They sure can't bear those old classics," I said. "No," she replied, "but they try!" Here was a very quick-witted lady who was always enjoyable to chat with, however briefly.

CHAPTER 20
We Need You Here Fifteen Minutes Before the Kids Arrive

Survey results for the question: "The high school would be a better school if ..." were:
> —you fired a few English teachers
> —we didn't have so many rules ... and every year it gets worse and we just keep on getting more rules!
> —we didn't have to come into school for electives like art.
> —there were no foreign languages.
> —we didn't always get screwed!
> —the arts program were cared about more. There is too much emphasis on sports, visual and performing artists should be recognized more.
> —everyone was treated the same, who cares if you're the mayor's nephew!
> —the whole town didn't know each other and we weren't all townies. For example, it would be better if my teachers didn't have my parents in high school. I think grading would be different in that case, some teachers are really biased.
> —days were shorter.

—people weren't so uptight and make things more fun for the students.

—we didn't have to go!!!

—does it matter? It wouldn't happen anyway because the voice of the senior class falls upon deaf ears in the administration.

—it was more organized.

—pit was actually a school rather than a prison!

—all policies were debatable and then allowed to have a democratic vote.

—the music program had more money and recognition.

—it didn't exist!

—seniors actually had privileges.

—there was smaller schools within a larger school.

—everyone was like Joey!

—all the energy they put towards rules and enforcing them went into teaching.

—we had real classrooms, real teachers, a fair administration, vacation days and real food!

—the teachers had their degrees and the administration helped rather than suppress.

—Mr. Doyle didn't retire.

CHAPTER 21
Not Everyone Should Be a Teacher

We make it look so easy, but not everyone is cut out to be a teacher. Take, for instance, Todd, who was hired to be an elementary music teacher, filling in for someone on a leave of absence. The position was just for one year, and that may have contributed to the fact that he was hired in late August one year, because more suitable candidates didn't apply.

I got a call from him very late one night, and would get many more as association president before all this was finished. He was a very good musician who wanted to teach after studying for eight years in music college. He was a very strange young man who really never understood what it took to teach.

Todd was like other music teachers who are driven to have their students prepare to perform in a concert; everything they do is directed that way. However, in attempting to get the best out of their music students, they seem to forget that students need to be brought along gently. Instead, Todd was sarcastic and mean to his students, so much so that they didn't want to come to school when music class was scheduled.

He was made aware by the school's principal that this was not to be the way he should operate.

He resorted to having students stand in the corner of his classroom on many occasions. Classroom management requires getting the students' attention and maintaining it for forty-five minutes. He obviously had no teacher-prep courses in music college, and had great trouble getting the attention of his students and maintaining momentum, so he resorted to these extreme disciplinary actions.

Once, he was giving individual attention to one student, at the expense of others ... and the whole school, as it turned out. You see, Todd had the student alone in the music classroom while he had the others—twenty-nine or so—wait in the hallway ... with their instruments ... until he called them back in. Needless to say, there was absolute bedlam in the corridor with third- and fourth-graders tooting their horns and banging their drums!

He was called into the principal's office about this, and agreed not to let it happen again. He was even given a mentor—a visual arts teacher—to help him, but he couldn't relate to her. I told him once to call the teacher he was replacing at her home, and she might help him with what worked for her in the past. He was warned that his type of thing had to end, and after a second occurrence, he was told that if it happened again, he would be terminated.

Todd called me and said he was very unhappy and wanted to know his rights. I explained to him that as a first-year teacher under the Education Reform Act, he didn't have any, and that he could be dismissed for no reason before Thanksgiving. It only got worse as the year went on. He accused the principal of listening to other teachers and believing lies, accusations, and false interpretations. He said that she used malicious, destructive, and abusive words toward him and attacked his professionalism(!) causing him to get unproductive at work and physically sick.

He was even seen leaving the building after a meeting with the principal and building representative from the association, and leaving his kids unattended until the director of music stepped in. Todd didn't fit in at the school, and I suggested that he seek out male teachers and get to know them in a sea of females—which is predominant in most elementary schools everywhere.

I had more reason to doubt his teaching ability when he called me and complained that he couldn't get to his materials because the janitors had put his music risers in front of his closet while cleaning his room. I suggested that as a man, he get over it and meet the janitors halfway, and help them move the risers out of the way so he could get to his supplies. He told me he wasn't doing physical labor like that for anything. I replied, "Well, it's your stuff and you need it, don't you?" I gave him a little word of advice I always used with the custodial staff, and that was to get them on your side from the first day, and you'll have everything you want. He could not see what good that would do!

He said he was very much a hard worker and had been at it for eight years and knew his stuff. I said, "Well, Todd, I've been at it for thirty-five years and I'm still learning!" Silence at the other end of the phone. He also told me he wanted to become involved in the teachers association and would be a chairman of a committee—if he could get paid. I explained that association work was usually volunteer, and he quickly lost interest after hearing it.

The principal called him in again after getting reports that he was beginning his classes by having the students shout out loud that he was the best music teacher in the whole wide world, and that he was playing totally inappropriate ZZ Top music in fourth grade—certainly not in any curriculum guide in the system!

He shouted back to the principal, and the building rep attempted to end the meeting because it was not in his best interest, but Todd walked out and left the building. I called the principal after hearing what transpired from my association liaison. I told her that we didn't want bad teachers in the system either, and to just be sure that he got his due process as dismissal came. She thanked he and was somewhat stunned that I wasn't defending him; but I couldn't and wouldn't.

In the spring, after the music concerts were done, he got the word that he was being let go. He would get a recommendation from the principal placed in his folder and have his health insurance paid by the school department for the rest of the school year and over the summer. He would be placed on medical leave of absence, and the system would tell other systems that he resigned and was not terminated. He would be allowed to collect unemployment until he got another job—somewhere!

Sad but true. Not everyone can teach, and it is the job of the school system and teachers' association not to protect them. The kids are the bottom line, and having this type of individual instructing them was very negative indeed.

CHAPTER 22
In Order to Graduate, Students Must Accrue Ninety-five Credits

Part of a teacher's recertification was to obtain 120 points in his field and general education in Massachusetts. This can be in courses, workshops, authorships, conferences, and teaching adult education, for example. I got various credits in courses but was given ten credits for attending the second Clinton presidential inauguration in 1997 and four credits for attending the dedication ceremonies of the Franklin D. Roosevelt Memorial in Washington, D.C. in 1998. Other things were for National Education Association conferences I went to and "effective teacher" training courses. Not too bad for a veteran like me, but absolutely essential just the same to keep up in professional development. God help us if we don't keep abreast of the latest trends and theories!

I gave up on chaperoning student dances sometime in the 1970s, and I'll tell you why. Having arrived to have a good time and do my duty, I quickly found someone throwing up in the bleachers in the gym where the dance was being held, and two others trying to knock down the gym wall while heavily on drugs. When one boy took the window pole and proceeded to break the windows in the boys' lavatory because we wouldn't let him back in the gym once he left, that was enough for me. Along with another teacher, I found my coat and threw it out the gym window into the parking lot below where I had parked, and quickly left the affair. Students continually asked me to chaperone again and again, but after I told them my story, they got the message.

Nothing is as horrible as the death of a student in one's class or of one who you have taught. A teacher does not see the finished product, but he is nurturing the child, and when that child dies, it is very unfair. One such death occurred less than ten years into my career, when a young boy died of respiratory trouble. I had to change the seats of all the students in the classroom the next day after the funeral. I could never stop seeing him sitting up back by the window each time that particular class met. Some time later, the editor who had the yearbook dedicated to me died after she completed nursing school. She was a very bright young lady, but never fulfilled her true place in society. I have often said that teaching is the only profession that brings two different generations together to complete the job. How fortunate teachers are, no matter how painful sometimes.

One really has to be careful, for you never know who is sitting in front of you as students. I have taught kids who went on to be a mayor of the city, city councilors, school committee members, and a county sheriff. At one reunion I was invited to attend, one boy came up to me and said, "You almost told me off when you were my teacher, didn't you?"

I replied "Yes, Steve, I almost did!" He told me that next Saturday he was taking his bar exam on his way to becoming a lawyer! I told him that was wonderful and wished him good luck. You never know, because the last a teacher sees of his students in high school is as they graduate at the ripe old age of eighteen. They have their whole lives ahead of them.

Over the course of my career, I was fortunate to receive at least two T.I.P. grants—standing for Teacher Initiative Program—from my local school system. One was for the theatre arts program that I began to replace the defunct senior plays in the late 1970s, and the other was for a law course I brought into the curriculum in my department in the early 1970s. The former was for updating the drama program and expanding it to something truly worth the talented students we had. Both were worth $1,000 each, and it was spent directly on the programs.

One of our goals as teachers is to make sure students can take notes in preparation for college. My lectures were in outline form, and I expected students to be able to follow me and write down good notes from them. Once, while lecturing on the Vietnam War in the 1970s, as I walked back and forth in front of the class, I happened to notice that one student was doodling. I stopped and told him that I thought he should be writing down what I was presenting to the class and not drawing. I could see as I stood over him that he had quite elaborate drawings with bombs being dropped on a map of Vietnam.

Thinking I had to make an example of him to others in the class, I told him to read back to me what I just said in my lecture. With great caution and expertise, he proceeded to read back almost verbatim what I had just said. I was flabbergasted! Later I learned that he was a visual learner, and that was how he took notes in almost all his classes.

Years after his graduation and attending art school, he was hired by the local newspaper, where he is today as their political cartoonist, and his drawings appear pretty often on the editorial page. He is wonderful as a caricaturist of local leaders like the mayor, as well as drawing national politicians. He can also use his talents to sum up in a few panels just what the editorial itself is professing in words.

So, as a teacher, you just never know who's sitting in front of you, or what they will do with what they learned in high school!

When I worked with the music teacher putting on our ten musicals together, we often visited other high schools in the area when they were doing a show we might do in the future. We were after ideas, as well as to see how students and their teacher directors treated the material.

Once we learned that a nearby high school was doing the Lerner and Lowe classic "Camelot". We often thought of doing this great musical, so we made plans on a Friday night to go and see it. We called for tickets and reserved two seats. We got settled in the school's "cafe-torium" (combination cafeteria and auditorium)—not the best situation and we were lucky we didn't have to deal with such a setting in our high school.

The overture started and then King Arthur appeared in a painted cardboard tree that just didn't look realistic since the audience could see it was corrugated cardboard..The student playing Lancelot appeared on stage shortly after, and I was just taken aback by how handsome he was. Obviously, this was why he was cast in the part, but once he started to sing, I knew it wasn't because of anything else. The boy started to belt out "C'est Moi," and he got just a few lines sung when it was obvious to me and others that he had a lisp! What came out sounded like "they moi" instead of what it should have been. I was laughing quietly but soon couldn't contain myself. The music teacher had her hand to her mouth to muffle the sound she was trying to contain. It only got worse as the number went on. The audience, for the most part, must have known the boy, because they were very patient with their muted laughs.

I whispered, "I think I'll have to go." I got the eye of agreement from my music teacher friend, and we stayed until the number ended and the applause came. All the way home and for years later, we just broke up laughing anytime someone asked us if we were ever going to do "Camelot".

Funny Test answer-

What were the 14 points by Woodrow Wilson?

Answer- The number he scored when he was at Princeton.

(Correct answer- His contribution to the Treaty of Versailles that ended World War I.)

CHAPTER 23
Pay Close Attention to This!

Time is of the essence these days, and nowhere is it lacking more than in teaching. Everyone is after teachers' time. How much is enough? How many classes can teachers teach and not be out of contract? This especially applies on the high school level, where courses are much more in depth than any other level. It is absolutely imperative that certain things are understood by all involved.

If a teacher is a history major, like I was, how many courses can he be expected to teach before he is out of contract? The standard answer to this question was two subjects and three preparations. Huh? Let's examine these definitions as stated in our contract, and it will point out even more silliness involved in public education today!

A discipline is a field of study or specific body of knowledge like social studies, mathematics, science, foreign language, and English.

A subject is a department of learning or a subdivision of a discipline, such as American history, algebra, French, chemistry, and British literature.

A preparation or "prep" is a subject and/or level of a subject that requires a period of time for a teacher to prepare and develop a different lesson plan, like American history advanced placement, American history honors, French I, French II, French III, Geometry honors, Geometry college level.

A class is a group of students scheduled at a specific time to study a specific subject like American history during first block or period in the day.

A section is a subdivision of students assigned to a teacher for a specific subject at a specific time in a school schedule, such as American history honors when there is more than one of the same class being offered during a year, semester, and/or quarter.

Are there any questions?

Let's take a look at two real scenarios:

First, my case for almost fifteen years or so was that I taught three social studies classes and three theatre arts classes. By all accounts, I was "out of contract" but I did it, and the administration knew I would—because I didn't want the drama classes to die. No one else would teach them, so I did. Once or twice, the principal was "nice" and gave me no other duties like homeroom or study hall or lunchroom duty, but over the years, that wore off when staff cuts happened. I was forever forced to climb the stairs to the third-floor social studies classrooms, and then go down them to the auditorium to teach the theatre arts classes. For a while, I had my social studies classes in a classroom near the auditorium, but that wore off too when the math department wanted their room back! I eventually gave up the drama classes and they hired a part-time teacher. When I retired, they were on their third replacement for me in the field, and that felt very good!

The second example would be a science teacher new to the profession who volunteered to teach five different classes and have five different preps. When I heard about this, as association president, I was livid. If he would do it, then the administration might arm-twist others to do it too. Eventually, he saw the light, and before I retired, he was obviously burned out and finally knew the meaning of contract language to protect the teacher:

"No teacher will have more than two subjects to teach or three preps to undertake."

Another funny answer I got on a test was in responding to
Identify- Rough Rider Teddy Roosevelt
"Teddy Roosevelt was a rough rider--the horse didn't like him very much!"

At a faculty meeting early in my career I remember we had the Home Economics Co-Ed classes provided what we thought were delicious brownies as refreshments.

The next day almost everyone complained how sick they were that night.

It seemed someone had laced the brownies with........ Ex-lax!

CHAPTER 24
See, Scream, Do by Example—but Don't Touch!

He came to me and said, "You should know as association president that I am suspending Ernie for five days, due to a touching incident." The principal didn't mean something nice and tender. He meant that one of our teachers had been accused by one of his students of inappropriate behavior unbecoming a teacher.

I made my way to the principal's office, and Ernie was already there. He was as quiett dazed. The principal calmly explained that a young girl had accused him of touching her many times, in and out of class, and that she didn't want to be in his class anymore.

Before Ernie was told to leave the school and go home, I told him that I would contact the Massachusetts Teachers Association legal department, and I asked for his home phone number. In light of all that had been in the news about the scandals in the Catholic Church, I was very concerned.

What had happened was very innocent, and could be taken two ways. Ernie had used the girl as an example of a lesson part he needed to convey something to the students, and in front of them all, actually picked her up bodily. Another instance happened out of school, when the student needed help getting up some steps, and he put his hand under her arm and assisted her.

This little girl was having trouble as a teenager, and she sought Ernie out for aid. After school hours, he spent time with her alone and with her girlfriends in his classroom, discussing life. When she wrote poems to him as he checked in her notebook, he ignored them and passed them off as typical teenage scribbling.

So it came to pass that guidance switched her out of Ernie's class after she had her mother intervene, and after she made a big deal out of the whole thing in her guidance counselor's office. Counselors must take action, because they never know if it is indeed serious. Finally, after not having Ernie any longer as her teacher, I said that she made the accusations to get attention. She missed him.

The state's child advocacy department stepped in, and in one of our meetings—again in the principal's office—told us that while it didn't appear to be anything sexual here, they had to investigate, especially in this day and age. Ernie was devastated and continued to be out of school on an extended paid administrative leave.

Students got wind of what was going on, and started e-mailing him at home, both supporting him and chastising him. I called him daily and suggested that he prepare lessons and send them in for his substitute. I also told him not to sit and brood about it, and to do something physical like go for a walk or chop wood.

One day, we were called to the principal's office again, with lawyers for both sides, but not the girl or her mother. The state authority read a detailed report that he was satisfied that nothing had happened for legal pursuit. Then two policewomen entered the office. Upon sitting down, one stated that if she stayed, anything said by anybody from now on could warrant the reading of the Miranda warning! I was speechless and scared shitless. Nothing in dealing with the soccer affair the previous year had upset me as much as this did. Our lawyer requested that the police wait outside under these circumstances, and that he would deal with them separately. With that, they got up and left—thank God.

In the meantime, scuttlebutt ran rampant in the faculty lounge. Where was Ernie? Why was he out of school? Did the local press know what was going on? Would this hit the papers like the soccer incident? A joint press released was given to the paper one day after the principal got a phone call from them inquiring about it. I sat with Ernie until five o'clock one Friday afternoon as the administration prepared to cover their respective asses. They were concerned about the school and the child. Nothing was said about poor Ernie sitting there. I interjected and said that something must be put in the press release that the teacher was innocent.

It was over, and Ernie was re-instated, and no one actually knew what had transpired. No one knew what I went through to keep it from exploding like the soccer incident. Hadn't we learned anything yet? Yes, as I told the staff in my newsletter, but don't ever touch a student— period. Many teachers don't realize that times have changed, and that they could be in court at the drop of a hat. Teachers are unique, but they don't realize how very vulnerable they really are.

It is now a very sad day in education, when teachers can't reach out and touch somebody because it could be taken the wrong way. But the day has arrived everywhere that teachers can't do the job like they used to or probably want to. With this incident, some now know better, especially Ernie.

CHAPTER 25
When You're Out, You're Out

I t happens occasionally in the school year that a teacher has to be out of school for one reason or another. The majority of the time out is for illness, but there are other things that happen, warranting a teacher to be absent. Conferences, conventions, personal days, and what is known in the teachers' room as "mental health." These days are when everything just piles up and the teacher needs to be out to re-energize his batteries.

Substitute teachers are called in to cover classes when the regular teacher is not there. Lesson plans have to be left or called in so the kids will have something to do and learning goes on. Upon returning, the teacher gets a report as to what transpired in class when he was absent. One such report I got stated that the kids were good and they worked on the assignment left. Some kids had trouble finding their way back to class and took advantage of the sub, I thought. I dealt with them upon my return and marked in my rank book to give them a "demerit" when figuring out their quarterly grade.

Sometimes, unthinking teachers left nothing for the sub, or say they have plans that couldn't be located. Kids loved to write phony names on the attendance sheet, and the sub soon learned not to call out the names when checking for accuracy. Such names as "I.M. Pregnant" or "Dick Hurts" or "Dick Trickle" are obviously not to be said orally in a mass of teenagers when checking attendance! Most subs are dedicated people who can get dressed in two minutes and appear in school, ready to go if called in the early hours of the morning.

Our subs are called by a secretary who is in charge of the calling for the entire school. Some systems have agencies they go to, or they have an administrator do it. Pay is really a slap in the face, because nothing could be worth the aggravation they endure to come into a school and be at the mercy of teenagers today.

My classes always knew that if they raised hell when I was out and drove the sub crazy, I would deal with them very severely upon my return. For the most part, I experienced no serious problems, but I was most frustrated when I left stuff and the sub didn't teach it, or the sub was from a different field than history and expounded on that for the duration of the day and wasted everybody's time in the long run.

My personal outlook regarding subs was that they were just that. They didn't know how I taught the class or what was necessary to be successful in my shoes. Occasionally, subs were discontented teachers who were looking for work and figured that if they got on the sub list, they had a foot in the door. This sometimes worked, and sometimes it didn't. Depending on the administration at the time, some subs never got beyond that status and were considered to belong there, and were not to be brought on the faculty.

Subs are needed in schools, and many actually hire permanent subs every year. Once a sub is in for a month, they usually are placed on salary, but they may not be. It may be cheaper for the school system for just pay them $100 a day and forget the benefits like health insurance if that is the case.

I have seen some wonderful people who sub almost daily, and I always greeted them as the "all-American sub"! Subs can tell you who the kids like, who they hate, and who is doing what in class. I always thought that the administration would be wise to interview them halfway into the school year, to see what they perceive in the school as impartial outsiders. I thought they would really get an unbiased and unique earful and helpful advice for the good of education. Their excuse would probably be lack of time, but for the good of everybody involved in public education, my advice to them is—find it!

Another actual answer to a test question I recieved years ago-

"How big was William Howard Taft's administration?"

William Howard Taft was the biggest president we ever had and got stuck in the White House bathtub until a law was passed to make them larger!

CHAPTER 26
This 'n' That

After grading and rating students for what seems like forever, I asked them to describe themselves for me. These kids were seventeen and eighteen, and the best all-around youngsters anyone could ever encounter. Here are their answers to the question:

"Describe yourself so I can include you in the book I am writing about my teaching career."

—your favorite student—the kid you never want to remember, but you never forget!

—sarcastic, creative, I dominate!

—outgoing, fun

—hot, loud and cool!

—German exchange student

—I am me!

—loud

—dashing with rugged good looks and a winning smile, oh, yes, I had it all!

—energetic, willing, and I can put a smile on a lot of people's faces.

—hot, cool—and I get my work done!

—your favorite student who was here for every class!

In order to run a successful class, but more importantly, in order to reach these students, I asked the following question on a pre-semester survey, and here are their responses to:

"Name one thing you do NOT want to happen in the class in order to be successful and pass it."

    —group activities that allow most to slack off and copy while you do the work!

    —a lot of homework

    —lectures = failures; discussion = success!

    —huge writing papers

    —I don't know.

    —oral presentations

    —student presentations

    —get below and 85 average so I don't have to take the final!

    —hmmmmm … … …

    —having a lot of homework.

    —too much order!

    —homework and projects

    —public nudity!

    —failing

    —too many tests— more projects

    —getting a bad grade

CHAPTER 27
Your Spelling Is Atrocious!

In a word, students cannot spell anymore. They are forever tied these days to the spell check on their computers to bail them out, but where are their computers when they take a test? I have always been a champion of correct spelling, probably since Miss Lord gave me an A in spelling in grade eight. I believe that being able to spell correctly is a sign of an educated person. While spelling has gone the way of geography in public schools—not being taught separately as a subject—we must foster correct spelling to save our culture and civilization, as well as making our students better learners.

What causes this spelling problem? For one thing, students watch too much television and pick up spelling injustices from commercials that call for big "sellabrations" in stores, and think that because they see it that way on television, then it must be right.

The influx of foreign children into our society and schools has contributed to spelling being infringed upon in education. Or, for instance, take the brilliant(!) idea many teachers promote to "just write and don't bother with the spelling—you can correct that later." This idea is preposterous. Kids never get to correct it, and the damage is done in their minds. Still, we have the leaders in education who promote this "creative spelling"—wrong from the get-go and absolutely an injustice to their students.

In my history class, I was always asked "Does spelling count?" to which I answered "No, but I always circle the errors and take that into consideration in my final grading of your essay." I was adamant that students spell historical names and events correctly, because it was part of learning the subject matter. If they take French, they must learn to spell correctly in that language, so why not in history too?

I am always calling attention to misspelled words in newspapers, magazines, and even road signs! The state of New Hampshire has put out signs advertising that no "alcohlic" beverages are allowed on their beaches, when it should read "alcoholic." Despite my letters to the governor, the signs still haven't been changed! One time, we stopped at a car wash, and when we were done, we went to use the vacuum and I noticed it was "avaiable"—no l between the i and the third a. I almost left, I was so disgusted. The same for a restaurant that served oysters Rockerfeller instead of oysters Rockefeller. If they can't spell the name correctly, how in the world can they prepare it correctly?

An old spelling rule like "i before e, except after c"—with exceptions— is still a foundation of good spelling education. Teachers tend to side with the students by saying the exception like the spelling of the word "science" throws that out—so kids believe the teacher and never learn such aids to their education, which would actually help them when in doubt.

I believe that if students did more reading and cut down on the television viewing, they would become better spellers. Seeing it in print would be almost synonymous with this generation of visual learners, and they would benefit enormously.

In history, I always loved the "creative spelling" mishmash my students made of these terms and names, to name a few:

—inauguration - the swearing in of the US president

—assassination - the murdering of a politician
—Khrushchev - the Soviet Union's cold war premier
—Bush - the president (not Busch the beer!)
—definitely, not definately
—business, not buisness
—college, not collage (You can't go unless you can spell it right!)
—controversy, not controversay

Since I taught history, my students complained quite often that they learned more English in my class than in English class. Yes, I would reply, when courses in that other department are entitled American "literature" or British "literature" instead of English or language arts, you know where their emphasis is lies, so I had to drill correct spelling for all it was worth!

I always was and always will be part of the "spelling police" in this country and be proud of it!

CHAPTER 28 ———————
The Play's the Thing

Over seventeen years of my thirty-seven-year career, I was involved in producing and directing what I considered twenty-five different unique and educational high school shows. Eleven were musicals and fourteen were straight plays. The overall objective was to provide good theatre and a professional experience to high school students who took part in them. Theatre is a valuable learning vehicle for all kids, and those who came out for the shows always stood out in my mind as kids who got a lot more out of high school beyond the normal book learning. They also had a different respect for me, as I was with them in producing something everyone needed to do their fair share on or it wasn't going to happen. They also liked to see me on weekends in dungarees, getting down with them, painting scenery and eating lunch beyond the normal classroom setting.

My first straight play was Neil Simon's "Plaza Suite", a three-act comedy that I did with three different casts. This actually came as a result of a class project in theatre arts. The students were having such a good time, they suggested that they do this production for an audience. As a result, it started another tradition of producing two plays a year instead of just a musical, which I had established three years earlier. Sometimes as I watch the movie on television, with Walter Matthau playing the three male leads, I realize how great my kids did with the same material. I can still quote lines from the play and enjoy the rapid humor delivered with America's premier playwright's fabulous style.

The next year, we did "Arsenic and Old Lace", which I already described in these pages. It was so well done and similarly so well written that the kids performed sensationally.

Agatha Christie's "The Mousetrap", the longest-running play in the world, was next. The cast did a fine job with keeping the audience guessing as to who was the villain until the very end. I had a funny thing happen after I cast that show. Once we had the read-through on a Friday afternoon, many kids told me that they couldn't take on such a big show and either asked to be recast or dropped out completely! So that night, in the high school gym, there was a dance being held, and I went and actually recast the show with the kids there who had auditioned and received other roles. It was a riot, and it worked very well, since rehearsals were set to begin on Monday and I couldn't waste any more time if I was to pull this off in eight weeks!

That was followed by "The Man Who Came to Dinner" by Kaufman and Hart—a classic of the American stage and screen. It had a very large cast, due to great student interest, and one student carried the old theatre adage of "break a leg" a bit far, as she got hurt skiing and did unfortunately break her ankle. Hence, she played the maid while on a walking cast, and the audience actually thought it was part of the play!

Noel Coward's "Blithe Spirit" is an English parlor drama that I picked for the fifth fall show. The great writing and character development aided the kids pulling this masterpiece off without a hitch. One problem was the makeup of the deceased wife who comes back from the dead. She started out looking like a Smurf, until we toned down her makeup as the play's opening night approached!

The administration was really piling it on with my rugged schedule, and so I took a two-year hiatus until they were more conciliatory. I was young and energetic, and made it look like such fun; no one realized that to see a show as an audience member for two hours actually took months of hard work. All this was done while carrying on my usual five classes in two different departments—social studies and theatre arts, and assorted duties. Kids kept asking me to do another straight play, and had approached the administration for me. No one since then has had the schedule I endured, with social studies as well as theatre arts classes to do a show and work with the music teacher to do a school musical, too! I might add that when I retired, the school was on its third drama teacher to do the work I did for seventeen years, as a matter of fact.

I chose "You Can't Take It with You"—another great American contemporary classic with which to make my directing re-appearance. It was well received and the kids did another masterful job with this tremendously funny three-act comedy. It really stands the test of time, and is respected today as well as when it was first on Broadway.

We were back to Agatha Christie again after that with her splendid "Ten Little Indians" mystery romp the following autumn. That was fun and had the audience guessing until the very end again as to "whoooo dun it?" No movie of this material has ever been made that does it justice, in my opinion. Why the producers feel they must change the locale as Christie wrote it I will never understand. I worked so hard on this one, I passed out at the cast party due to extreme physical exhaustion. After a few days at home, I went back to school but realized that it was really getting to me to keep up this pace of teaching two different subjects and doing two shows each year.

"The Pink, Panther Strikes Again" that starred Peter Sellers,was the spoof I picked for a large number of kids again who wanted to be part of the show. The lead and all the cast were well rehearsed and excellently suited for their parts. I pulled a real fast one by having a generic set used for multiple scenes, and it cut down on the production problems a lot.

The old-fashioned "The Cat and the Canary" mystery was another superb hit the next fall. The whodunit bug struck again, and the audience was spellbound by the actions on the stage during this stunner. Mistaken identities, revolving bookcases, dramatic lighting, and mature students capable of handling this material made it one of my very favorites of all the shows I did.

I love "Harvey", with Jimmy Stewart in the movie, but shied away from it, due to its dual set requirement. Finally I realized that I was not going to be doing many more shows, so why not? We pulled it off with a set on wheels, and even an appearance of the six-foot rabbit in the curtain call of this three-act comedy. The moral lesson learned was that if people are happy in their own way, who are we "normal" people to question them?

I also always wanted to have high school kids do "Charley's Aunt", ever since I read it in college. The big problem there was the period costumes we needed, so with a costume company in a nearby town, I went whole hog and rented whatever we needed, and it was splendid. The kids and audience loved this old chestnut! The gender-bending, cross-dressing spoof was a delight for high school boys to endure.

Children's theatre is probably just as hard to do as Shakespeare, but I wanted to do "Hansel and Gretel" in the worst way, so we did it. I appealed to the local adult theatre group for help with this one, and found a very competent assistant director who was wonderful to work with. I was able to step back and let him work with the kids and special effects needed in this fairy tale. The witch and the oven and the whole children's story fascination was readily accepted by all.

At long last, I announced that I couldn't do the plays anymore, as the administration wanted me strictly as a history teacher. The last play I picked mark the occasion was "Up the Down Staircase" based on the riotous Belle Kaufman nonfiction book. Everyone had such fun gently slapping the faculty and school insanity without getting into big trouble. As the curtain closed and I had done my twenty-fifth and final show for the high school, I was mighty glad in many ways.

I loved this part of my career tremendously, and have many, many wonderful memories of kids who went above and beyond the norm to work with me in this special aspect of public high school education.

Another actual test answer-
How are John F. Kennedy and Robert F. Kennedy related?
Answer- Father & Son
(Correct answer- Brothers)

CHAPTER 29
Highlights from NTA Newsletters

Communication is vital as a teachers' association president. I used to put out a monthly newsletter, in order to keep all the teachers informed about things going on that should concern them. It was my way of trying to make up for years of no communication from other presidents. As I learned at presidential training sponsored by the Massachusetts Teachers Association my first summer pre-inauguration, if you want the troops to support you, you had better keep them informed as to what was going on.

So, over the years, usually at the beginning of each month, I put out a one-page newsletter, printed on both sides and written exclusively by me. I printed it on bright pastel-colored paper in order to stick out from the humdrum white paper our bulletins were usually printed on. I ran it off and then relayed it to my five building representatives in all our schools. The feedback was very encouraging, and one year, when I only produced it every other month, teachers told me that they missed it not coming out monthly. A few teachers loved to pick out spelling and grammatical errors, but at least I knew that they were reading it if they were that concerned about what was in it!

I called it "The Paperclip," since our high school athletic logo was the clipper ship, and I just thought the name worked for bits and pieces of information teachers could read. I never gave it to the administration, but it was fascinating how quickly we got action on something if they got wind of it in the newsletter! The same could be said for the monthly minutes every teacher also got. The administration had the balls to take it out of the teachers' mailboxes and read it to find out what we were up to. Once, a member even asked me to put all correspondence of this type in sealed envelopes, but I didn't have the time, and besides, I sort of liked the idea that they were actually reading my monthly periodical.

In the first year, under "Presidential Patter" I wrote:

It has come to my attention that some people are having problems adjusting to an active union after years of inactivity. This is what I ran on, folks! I have said all along that we should be "proactive and not reactive." Many of you have said "right on." Now that we are doing this, I think we all have to realize that this a violent departure for Newburyport! I do not intend for us to become militant, and if a few of you are perceiving my actions to be that, then that is a problem you are incorrectly having!

I invite you to any executive board meeting to voice your complaints. We meet every first Thursday each month at the high school, starting promptly at 3:30 PM. These meetings are open to each and every one of the members. The last meeting ran until 5:30 PM! We are building our association up to something that I thank all officers and board members for working on so long and hard! For a great majority of you, I thank you for your continued support and good words! I sincerely appreciate your kindness and advice.

In my second year, the following appeared:

We are extremely pleased to announce that the Newburyport Teachers Association will be making a sorely needed donation to the Newburyport Police Department. In the name of public safety, the NTA Executive Board has purchased a defibrillator for the Newburyport Police that will be used in resuscitating heart attack sufferers. Each of the four police cruisers will now have its own machine with this gift. We know you will all agree that this gift in the spirit of humanitarianism could benefit all the citizens of Newburyport tremendously!

In the third year of my presidency, I wrote:

This year will be the start of an exodus from this profession of some people who have taught here for over 30 years each. It is the beginning of the end of a terrific group who made the high school what it is and what it was to many in the community. When the city's population thought of NHS, they associated practically everything it stood for by this group of teachers, coaches and great overall folk.

It is really a bittersweet time for everybody but nothing lasts forever and there comes a time to say goodbye. To think of the high school without these teachers is almost incomprehensible! Adding all their years of teaching together is over 275 total years in public education!

All the new people who will fill their jobs for them may take over their classes, mailboxes and parking spots but they will never replace them. Anyone who thinks these guys can be replaced hasn't been around too long or doesn't have too much gray matter between their ears!

Caring, dedication, responsibility and tradition embodied by these teachers will be sorely missed by everybody who taught with them and who were lucky enough to have them as friends.

Thanks, gentlemen, for being here and staying for most of your careers and lives. Newburyport High School loses tremendously with your departure. Best wishes for long, happy retirements. You all have earned them!

In the last year of my presidency, a sample of the newsletter can best be shared with this:

Four years are over and I am through as NTA president. I believe I have made a sizable difference in that short time and advanced the Association in its Herculean effort to provide the best possible services and protection for all the teachers in Newburyport. We have done many outstanding things during this time. No one can do it all by himself and I am especially grateful for the fabulous support I have received from the great majority of us. Whenever I called, you answered. You have been the backbone of the Association and to be your president for two short terms is something for which I will be ever grateful.

In my tenure, I have learned that it is absolutely impossible to please everybody. Instead, I listened, I acted, I watched, I responded, I offended a few, I did my best. I hope you were somewhat satisfied with the job that I did because if you think you can do better, then run! I was never involved in the Association until I realized that if I ran for office I might be able to do things differently. I now understand why things are the way they are. If I hadn't done this service for NTA, I never would have had the well-rounded teaching career from which I am now retiring.

I appeal to everyone on our staff to come forward and get involved in some small way. You can only benefit yourselves. Thank you very much for everything you have done for me. I offer my best wishes for continued successful teaching careers as you do battle with those who administer the dictums debatable education legislation. Don't let them unravel or dismantle your very core of teaching—the classroom—where teaching and learning emanate so beautifully daily from each school in the Newburyport Public School System. You truly do very outstanding work—keep it up!

Upon election four years ago, I received a book as a gift, and I offer the following from the source as I bid you all adieu—"Being president is like riding the back of a tiger!"

CHAPTER 30
High School & Kids Need Your Vote

After going down to defeat two years previously, the high school renovation project was put on the ballot again for citizen approval to a tax override. I got involved and wrote the following for the local newspaper:

Thirt five years ago, I began teaching in Newburyport. We had a wonderful high school full of school spirit and full of more than 1,000 students. Eventually new schools were built like Triton and Whittier and our enrollments shrunk. Over the years our faculty and curriculum changed considerably, but the structure did not. Our principals changed, our house plan came and went, and many of our fellow teachers left or retired. Except for a "cosmetic" facelift in the mid-1970s, NHS is still the same school.

Some of the students I had when I first started teaching came back this week as parents to our Open House. As they roamed the familiar hallways, they found that a few of the veteran teachers like myself were still there but that there were many new faces on the faculty. Many recalled sitting in the same seat in the same rooms when they went to NHS.

Neighboring schools like Amesbury High School and Pentucket are relatively new compared to NHS. We were calling the wing erected in the mid-1970s "new" then and we are still calling it "new" today. It is the only real physical improvement made to the high school, and it was added 37 years ago!

This November the citizens of Newburyport will be asked to approve a $34 million renovation to the school. They will be asked to consider making NHS a truly modern facility capable of use well into the 21st century. Our students need this "shot in the arm" desperately. They perform quite well on state exams and go on to good colleges. With a new structure, imagine how much better they could achieve!

The Commonwealth of Massachusetts will reimburse the city 68% of the cost of the project. The citizens of Newburyport will just have to pay 32% of the renovations! What a great bargain. Two years ago it would have cost less but it was defeated when it was placed on the ballot. Now we have it up for approval again. If it is defeated this fall, it will cost the city dearly. If we try again two years hence, costs will rise and the price will be far higher.

In about three years, NHS will undergo a massive accreditation again by the New England Association of Secondary Schools and Colleges. They will see that all the suggestions for improvement have been made except one—the structure itself. Nothing has been done since that report was done in 1993. This time we could actually lose accreditation if we don't improve the physical plant.

As president of the Newburyport Teachers Association, I appeal to all the citizens of Newburyport, whether or not you are graduates of Clipper City High, to vote for the renovations in November.

You may point with pride at the beautiful building as you drive by, but we all know it is only skin deep! Inside requires your affection, too. A first-class school inside and out is what we need. The kids who do so well on and off the athletic fields deserve it. The future parents who want their children to go to NHS deserve it. The city of Newburyport should want to reward our efforts as teachers and parents to provide for the future by voting in the affirmative come November.

In the election, the renovations were passed by more than 700 votes and the renovations commenced in September 2000.

CHAPTER 31
Why Are You Leaving?

There comes a time when a teacher chooses to leave the system for one reason or another. In recent years, we had so many leaving the high school particularly that many people asked me, as association president, to do an exit poll and find out why. A few years ago, I did, and here are the reasons for people choosing to bail out:

1) "The reason given for my departure was officially stated as 'position eliminated.' I strongly feel that the Superintendent had the last say. Also, the grievance filed by another teacher was upheld which made me lowest on the seniority list and I was let go. But given the happenings last year when another staff member was let go after twenty-five years, I truly believe that they do see my old department as fitting into the 'private school' they are creating instead of a comprehensive high school."

2) Official reason-"Administrative changes are causing an across-the-board change in staffing to allow newly hired administrators to pick their own team."
Unofficial reason-"A certain part-time interim department head misunderstood my intentions when I initiated a meeting with our district supervisor. As a result, he went to

the principal and started a big time about how I don't follow protocol. Soon a social worker intern at another school in the system was interviewed for my job and shortly later I was not renewed."

3) "The opportunity of doing something else came at the time I experienced serious and severe conflict with an administrator who made it clear that things would get worse for me. It was time to leave."

4) "I enjoyed the students and colleagues but a certain administrator did not care for me honest openness and my love for the students. This person also lacks the knowledge as to what makes a successful class. I miss the students and faculty."

5) "My reason for leaving was simply a matter of wanting a change. While I was happy at Newburyport, I felt a burning desire to try to build a successful athletic team at a higher level."

6) "I was laid off after one year of employment. I was not evaluated at anytime after January. My position was eliminated."

7) "The teacher whom I replaced for one year returned from their leave of absence. My contract was not renewed even before course registration was completed and the budget decided. I had been strongly led to believe that a position would be made available the next school year."

8) "I left because I had a chance to get a position which doesn't even exist in Newburyport and I was tired of the lack of positive leadership."

9) "My contract was not renewed, the reason as it was explained to me being the word had spread that I was looking for work elsewhere and the administration wanted to fill my position as soon as possible. I was looking but that prompted me to definitely leave. I thought it was very rude and it was just another act that showed me how poor the school administration is. I was even asked by my supervisor to reconsider, to reapply, because they were having trouble

finding a new teacher, but the insult was enough for me. I am very happy in my new school. The difference is day and night. The administration here actually cares about its staff and there's little or no bickering."

10) "I left because my contract was not renewed for the following school year. I enjoyed the year that I was there. The teachers were friendly and easy to work with and I established a good rapport with the students. However, the administration was not the easiest to work with. The leadership tone and style made me feel uneasy at times. In the end, everything worked out for me. I enjoy my new job and am thankful for the experience I got by working in Newburyport. I wish the best for everyone and pray that things will get better for you."

11) "The beginning of the end of my tenure began with the administrator's decision to implement heterogeneous grouping—or what passed for it. Any discussion regarding the decision was after the fact; concerns regarding and arguments against it were met with condescension or were perfunctorily dismissed. In short, the administration had their agenda set in stone. In addition to their intransigence, I was unable to adapt my style to such a wide mix of student ability levels and to such activities as cooperative learning. In short, my enthusiasm for the classroom rapidly diminished: it was time for me to leave."

12) "My contract was not renewed because my job was eliminated in what I understand was an ongoing effort to eliminate the entire department. I do miss the fine teachers as well as the students; however, I would not now give up the positive and active support I enjoy in my new position."

13) "Leaving was a very sad thing for me to do. I always assumed I would retire from there. I got to the point where I felt I could no longer work for someone I felt I philosophically disagreed with. I felt the building was being run by someone with no leadership qualities. it was the leaders of the faculty who kept the ship afloat. I felt I was not being supported in

a program that was so needed by the students. I felt I was not valued, and I felt I was lied to often. It hurt me deeply to see how my colleagues were treated. I feel fortunate to have been hired by a good school system that supports and values my program. I also feel fortunate to have been given a second chance, because I thought I was going to have to leave education. God bless those who have hung in there. You are all much better persons than I!"

14) "In many ways, I loved teaching. I had many wonderful students, an incredible mentor, and support. My decision to leave was made easier by extreme difficulties. I had no one to help me with the mechanics of starting the school year. No one ever explained the simplest things to me like how to hand out textbooks or use the copy machine. All the difficulties of being a brand new teacher were complicated by being forced to teach with a program for which I received no formal training. I was linked up with someone who helped by very briefly eventually and told me I would be a failure.

The antagonism and conflict created by forcing the teachers to teach this program were costly. I developed insomnia as a result of being thrown into the middle of heated arguments between members of the department. I received numerous late night phone calls from people wanting to discuss the issue. I was already overwhelmed by my responsibilities as a teacher and I couldn't handle the additional stress.

I am sure that there are many other feelings and experiences I could share but I suppose that I have already shared too much. I can thank the school for the opportunity I had to grow as a teacher and clarify my dedication to the profession. However, I sorely regret the pain, anger, and large amount of money I spent on therapy after the trauma of struggling to succeed. Thank you for the opportunity to express my feelings. Feel free to share this letter."

CHAPTER 32
Back, but Not Forgotten

severely hurt my back in school in 1978, the day we were getting out for Christmas vacation. It happened when I leaned over to pull very heavy scenery for the third musical we were producing. I was attempting to move a big set piece called a wagon, attached to a rope, when I felt terrific pain in my lower back. I couldn't believe it. Somehow I made my way with extra caution down off the stage steps and sat very gingerly in an auditorium seat. No one was around, but finally another teacher came in and helped me up. I tried to walk up the aisle and it only got worse. I knew I had to go to the hospital, and he drove me. The X-rays—taken on an extremely cold metal table—revealed partial disc involvement. The teacher drove me home and two students drove my car following behind us. I was told to get in bed and rest.

I was planning to drive out of state for Christmas with my mother to Pennsylvania to visit my sister and her family. I couldn't go. During my convalescence, my mother flew down and I made plans to see a back specialist out of town. He admitted me to Salem Massachusetts Hospital for a few days to have a myelogram to test for a ruptured disc. I was told not to lift my head from the bed pillow or I would have a horrible headache, so I ate a tuna sandwich sideways on the pillow.

I was released and sent home after a few days. No operation was necessary, but I would still be out of school for two weeks at least. One day in the shower, I picked my leg up to get out of the shower, and I experienced the worst pain in my leg I ever felt anywhere! I made my way to my bed and called the doctor. He said it was the result of the back injury, and I had to stay in bed. On Martin Luther King Day in 1979, I experienced the worst day of pain in my life. I had a wicked headache that would not go away, and I was all alone. I couldn't even call anyone on the phone, it hurt so much. Finally, I managed to call my aunt toward the end of the afternoon, and she called my doctor to help me. I fell asleep and woke up periodically throughout the day, and I only had a washcloth and darkness with me all that day in bed.

I couldn't shave, so I let my beard grow into what developed into a nice nine-year one. I kept it well-cropped, and loved it. My family felt otherwise but were glad I was better, so they tolerated it. I had to walk every day for exercise and learned to lift with my legs and not arch my back. I bought free weights and developed a routine to keep the weight off by great effort and desire to heal myself.

Once I was back in school, the athletic director allowed me to use the whirlpool in the locker room during my free period. I started by walking three times around the gym each morning. I traded in my sports car for one with bench seats, since bucket seats were too low. I developed a love affair with my Boston rocker, to keep my back moving even while sitting. I went to the lake every day and did exercises underwater, weather permitting.

In the meantime, two weeks before opening night, I returned to school for the show. The music director had done this show before, so she conducted rehearsals and we had a great hit. Everything was covered by insurance and workmen's compensation, so that may be the best thing that happened with the whole thing.

This whole episode changed by life and how I lived, but I did not have to have back surgery—thank God!

This was in response to a test question as follows:

Describe cremation as done by the Nazis in World War II.

Answer- Cremation was when people were covered in cream and tortured.

CHAPTER 33
Bill's Impeachment and Dick's Resignation

The hardest part of teaching history is when it is being made in the headlines. Students jump to the conclusions that items in the news show how bad politics are and associate everyone with such scandal. Such were the two parts of my career when I had to cover in class the impeachment of Bill Clinton and the resignation of Richard Nixon. I had gone to the second inauguration of Clinton in 1997, and I thought the presidency reached its lowest ebb with Nixon.

Clinton was the first or second time I taught history backwards— that is, by starting in the present and going as far back as possible by June. I think I did it another time in the creative seventies. The impeachment of Clinton really left me no choice, because it was in the headlines, and despite the historical problem of not being able to teach history until fifteen years go by and events are truly historic, I threw caution to the wind and started in the present.

When I told my class this was how I was going to teach the course that semester, they really jumped at the chance of doing it. They had never gotten up to the present, and usually ended up with World War I, they told me. So I told them that was what we were going to do, but they would have to be responsible for a great deal of it because it wasn't in the textbook. Instead we would rely on the newspapers and the Internet. It really served as a way for me to teach two-fold: cover the Clinton current issue and have the kids learn about technology.

At one of the first classes, I laid down the groundwork of the topic by saying that we would discuss the Clinton/Lewinsky affair, but the language would have to be above what they might hear in the locker room. They agreed and off we went. The first discussion was going great. We covered the issue by talking about what an impeachment was and was not. You didn't kick the man out of office if you impeached him; that would be the job of the United States Senate if the changes of impeachment came to trial there. We were almost done, and I told the class the bell was about to ring, and a boy in the back yelled out, "What was the stain on the dress?" A girl down front saved the day by saying, "DNA"! I loved it. The whole unit took about a month, and I thought it was very successful.

Nixon was another story. We were in the turbulent seventies and the Vietnam War was still raging. I had been one of the Massachusetts voters who voted against Nixon in his landslide election of 1972. With a state-by-state score of forty-nine to one, he had won his second term. I had a bumper sticker on my car that stated "Don't blame me, I'm from Massachusetts." The Watergate affair was in the news, and I was into it big time because I knew he should and probably would be impeached. As the whole thing snowballed and one by one all the president's men could not put Nixon back together again, I was delighted. I presented the ways we could evict the man from office and got called to the superintendent's office. "Be sure you are teaching history and not just current events," he said. I told him this was history in the making and I was covering both! I wanted to see him out of office, and I got my wish in the great summer of 1974 when he resigned!

Both Clinton and Nixon should have been removed from office, in my opinion. My studnets hated Nixon, like the rest of the country, but they were very sympathetic to Clinton. "What's he done wrong? Is the country at war? Is the economy lousy? The whole country is doing what he's doing," they told me over and over. Apparently the Congress thought the same way, and he was saved by uncourageous senators who failed to remove him from the presidency. I told my classes what he did was morally wrong and they just didn't understand. Boy, had times changed, and were my students right.

I had voted for Clinton twice and had gone to his second inauguration. I am a lifelong Democrat not as one of my cronies used to tell the story that she was born a Democrat and baptized a Catholic but close. I still feel he should have been removed, and wish he was.

The seventies were a very difficult time in which to teach because of many things, but the biggest was undoubtedly Vietnam. One day I was walking down the hall to class and I could hear bells softly ringing. I kept on walking but turned and saw this teenage girl walking behind me and about to pass me. She was dressed in typical garb of the decade—a peasant blouse, dirty bell-bottomed blue jeans, wearing little granny glasses and sporting long, straight hair. Around her head were feathers and little bells held in place with a small leather band. "Peace, man," she said as she passed me and went on her merry way to class!

Values were really at stake, and what to teach that was relevant was being debated everywhere. I was bombarded with kids who were very suspicious of everything. They didn't like school and didn't want to do anything. They were, for the most part, anti-war and didn't know why except that people were getting killed and there was draft. We were severely put to the test as to how to approach our history curriculum.

It was exceedingly hard to teach about this great democracy when the democracy you were professing to be wonderful was falling on its face in Washington and around the world. I wrote a letter to Ted Kennedy, my Massachusetts senator in the 1970s, asking for more aid to education.

He fired back a letter to me saying there wasn't money for everything, and due to the Vietnam War, aid to public education had to be cut. Truly "guns or butter" I thought after I read the letter.

"Postholing" was the way we taught history in those days. We had various events, usually wars, that we hinged everything else on, like elections and cultures. I always told my students that I didn't care what they were politically—Democrat or Republican—as long as they could defend themselves. I encouraged them to have their opinions based on something besides a loud mouth!

I encouraged them a lot. I had great students as well as mediocre students. I also had some pretty horrible students, too, but my job was to teach them and get them through the courses of United States history and government that were required for graduation by the school system as well as the state. As one student told me, I was a teacher who didn't hold it against him if he didn't "get it" from last year's teacher. That is right, I took them from where they were to where I had to get them by June each year.

I did my best and … the rest, as they say, is history!

CHAPTER 34
Video Viewing

"Is that all you do—show movies?"

This generation of students could benefit greatly from videos in every single class they take. Teachers, likewise, could provide badly needed insight to their instruction if they would only get on board and not be so negative about this valuable classroom aid.

"Another video? Every time I walk by your class, you're showing something!"

That's right—I was utilizing what a generation was raised on namely television and arcade games since they were born. Maybe there is a connection as to what they are learning, huh?

I have always incorporated videos, by whatever name they went, into my classroom instruction. Back in the '60s when I started teaching, I found filmstrips to augment my lectures and discussions. I found I had their attention then, and until I retired, I still had it. You must fully realize that videos must be part of the lesson and not just something used to fill a class period. Having taught for ninety minutes the last six years or so of my career, I could very easily have capitulated. I made my class take notes on videos or I had viewing guides for them to follow and pick up the points I wanted them to get from the video.

"I can't afford to take time from teaching to show a movie!" was uttered to me off and on my many of my colleagues.

Kids today are mighty bored by the sound of teachers' voices professing to know it all. Why not take advantage of the experts who know how to put it across and incorporate videos, films, or movies into your instruction?

For many years, I could only rely on filmstrips—out of date now—to bring videos into my teaching. Then, in the 1970s, I received a grant to run a movie course for students with learning problems in social studies. These kids were slow learners, and I designed a course with a ninety-minute period once week to show a film based on values like honesty, responsibility, trust, dedication, etc. I rented old sixteen-millimeter reel-to-reel Hollywood classics like "The Desperate Hours", "Shane", "The Caine Mutiny", "Dark at the Top of the Stairs", and subsequently had students relate the problems in the movies to problems they might encounter in life. What happened to the family in "The Desperate Hours" when the little boy didn't bring his bike in? What lessons did the child learn from his hero in Shane, the all-American Western starring Alan Ladd as he rode off into the sunset and the little boy cries out, "Shane, don't go, Shane!"

I had other vehicles of learning spring from video viewing, like reading. What great books incorporate similar themes, and what could students learn from them?

One thing to remember is that videos do NOT take the place of teaching. Videos only add to what you as a teacher must do to make your job successful. Many great videos exist that explain how to study successfully, how to be an A student, and how to grasp the three branches of the United States government. These are very useful and later I would only incorporate more entertaining videos once I found that they fit the circulum and not just killing time.

However, when I saw the Oscar-winning "Forrest Gump", I knew that what I was doing was absolutely right, and I show this fine flick every year, sometimes twice a year, once I reached the 1960s in my U.S. history curriculum. This assets of the movie are so obvious, but number one is that kids really relate to the actor Tom Hanks. The soundtrack with all the great music by the fabulous artists, from Joan Baez to Simon and Garfunkel, are not to be ignored either!

"Forrest Gump" has actual historical footage that was incorporated into the movie. When George Wallace is shown standing in the doorway of the University of Alabama, blocking the entrance of the two black students and thus defying national legislation, it says it all! The video message of hatred, bigotry, and racism in his face is something no history book could ever convey.

"What do you do after you turn the lights back on?"was a comment I heard from fellow teachers.

Discussion is usually centered around what kids saw and what is meant by certain parts of the video. Teachers who think I was just killing time were totally ignorant as to the greatness of videos in American education. Of course, social studies lends itself very well to this, perhaps better than all the other disciplines. One must keep in mind that while I lived through a lot of what I taught, from the Kennedy assassination to the Clinton impeachment, most students didn't. Therefore, what better way to relate than to watch a video? Someone once said something about a picture being worth a thousand words a while back, didn't they?

Other excellent videos for U.S. history are:

All the President's Men—for the Watergate affair.

Rebel Without a Cause—for the '50s and teenagers.

Quiz Show—for the TV cultural scandals in the 1950s.

The Graduate—for '60s sexual mores and coming of age.

A Civil Action—for fighting government corruption of the '80s.

Ghosts of Mississippi—for civil rights.

Wag the Dog—for presidential power and cover-up a la Bill Clinton.

Before a teacher begins, one must prep the class as to what they are about to see, without giving away the plot. If it's a well-known video, the class will already know what's coming. Be sure to ask for objections to foul language or risqué sexual overtones. Once my students heard me say this, they dismissed it by telling me that they heard worse in the school lavatories!

Success for teachers who work videos into their class will be achieved when the kids suggest videos they want to see. Be sure you check them and preview them ahead of time. "Pink Floyd–The Wall" is not suitable for the classroom, but "Ten Things I Hate about You" worked especially well in a sociology class I taught a few years ago.

You will need to procure your own VCR, as well as a room that can be darkened, if you are to be successful with videos. Also, be sure you mark down where you leave off for the next class, or you waste valuable time fast-forwarding! If you don't own the video, it costs very little to rent from Blockbuster, and they always give you a break if you tell them you are a teacher and showing the video in your class, should you fail to return it on time!

Video viewing—or video learning,—can tap into your visual learners' mode of understanding, just like regular teaching incorporates audio learners so well. Don't be afraid to use it, and don't be intimidated by the critics who wish they had thought of it before you did!

Above all, remember: You are using videos to enhance your subject area. Do not turn your course into video appreciation. That is not what you as a teacher were hired to teach, but you may appreciate videos more if you use them correctly to enhance your curriculum. You may actually be surprised to have someone say, "Can I borrow your video next class?"

CHAPTER 35

A Tribute to Former Students, Because You Never Can Tell Who's Sitting in Front of You

Over the years, I found it absolutely amazing how some of my students made out after high school. One day I was reading a theatre magazine, in my days (or daze) of teaching drama as well as history. There in print was a wonderful story of a former student of mine who was working very hard and successfully on Broadway as a costume designer!

As I read on, this girl was just sitting in a New York restaurant one day, sketching costume ideas on a paper napkin and was hired! Was I surprised? Yes. Was I shocked? No. Erika was an individualist in high school when I taught her. Twice I cast her, in supporting parts for two shows, "Arsenic and Old Lace" and "The Mousetrap", in which she played a policewoman and an old busybody respectively.

I always admired her originality, especially from the day she walked into my class with half the hair on her head dyed green and the other half dyed blue! Designing for a New York producer? Yes, and she did very well, too. I tried to contact her, to have her come back and speak to my theatre students, but was never successful.

Another time, there was a quiet boy who was in a very active class of outspoken young people. He always sat up front. He hardly said a thing but was a good student who was very easy to teach. Years later, after trying his hand at a number of jobs, he ran successfully for representative from our area to the State House and won. As time went on, he was picked by the governor to replace a corrupt sheriff and clean up the mess in Essex County, Massachusetts. He did a yeoman's job and ran for election and was victorious. I was so impressed, I donated to his campaign, and he was probably one of very few Republicans I ever gave money to, since I am a dyed-in-the-wool FDR Democrat! He has reformed the justice department in our county as its sheriff, and is a credit to himself and his family.

Over the years, he did come back to speak to my law classes in American government, to tell of his experiences. He never failed to thank me for being his teacher. I am so impressed with him; he is one success story I always told my students about. He could have run for lieutenant governor but turned his party down due to family commitments, and it was a smart move. Frank is a leader of our state's justice and criminal department and makes a fine impression.

There was one student of mine who was just incredible to work with behind the scenes of any production I undertook. This boy was really a master carpenter who was involved in the building of a ship set and a Model T car that actually was driven across the stage. Andy came from a wonderful family who were in the construction business. This enabled him to transfer his inherited abilities to help me in theatre immensely.

There was nothing we couldn't tackle with him as stage manager. He truly was a student who was able to contribute to the production and make it student-centered, on- and offstage. I always believed that the kids should have a total experience to see what was involved in the complete show. Andy once built the elaborate set for Arsenic and Old Lace with the very necessary full staircase for Teddy to run up and down and yell "Charge!" believing it was San Juan Hill.

Larry was in my very first class of American history. He was an outstanding student athlete and just an incredible kid to have in class. I found him a challenge and an interesting individual. He had it all. Just when I thought that I had covered everything, his hand would go up and he would ask a great question. I always thought that he would have made a great teacher/coach, but here was a young man who saw other opportunities in this country. He was the best high school quarterback I ever saw play the game. No one could run the option like this wonderfully talented person. He was to be a credit to his family and his school. To think that I had this type of individual as a first-year teacher made me mighty glad that I entered the profession. I never had another student who reached his level in anything.

A young woman was just the greatest to know and be in contact with as a teacher. She was so full of life and so full of enthusiasm that you just loved everything about her. She came from a large local family, and she has been a credit to them and herself. Kiki was fun to know and fun to teach. She was a great friend, and when I was retiring, I ran into her and she said that she couldn't believe it! She hadn't changed a bit, and was just as pleasant and thoughtful as ever. Any teacher would have been proud to have her as a student, because she was so totally involved. She was school spirit personified, and did a terrific job of getting everyone involved. She was a people person whom everybody liked. This was especially true of her teacher too.

When I retired, I received many notes and cards of best wishes, but there was one that stood out from all the others. It came from a former student of mine named Ghlee whom I taught in the seventies. She wrote to me stating among other things that students who were lucky enough to have me as a teacher benefited very much. She had such a pleasing smile and reserved nature about her that it made it a breeze to teach her. She was athletic and didn't want to have a career indoors, so she became a Peace Corps volunteer and a forest ranger. She was so good, she went on to train others. I had run into her a few times here and there after she was solidly entrenched in her career. I had many students over the years, but this young woman made it very lucky for me as her teacher to have her in my classes.

Very few students liked me well enough to call me "Dad," but this wonderfully talented girl did. Terri was very easy to teach and like. I had her in history classes as well as theatre classes, but it was on stage where this person was so terrific. I thoroughly enjoyed her each and every time she was cast in a role, be it in the straight plays or musicals. She holds the record of being in the most shows I was involved in. She performed for the joy of it, and audiences just loved her. She should have gone to Broadway, but she has her degree in nursing and is doing community theatre, I am very glad to know.

Once in a lifetime of a teacher a students comes along like Steve. He was my last yearbook editor in 1978 and was a unique individual to work with. While I was for doing something different and way out for a theme, Steve steered everyone back to a traditional yearbook with outstanding results. He went on to the U.S. Coast Guard Academy and made a career in the service. Over the years, I lost track of him then 9/11 occurred. To my surprise who did I see on television but Steve. He was in charge of directing the defense during this tramatic time in U. S. History. He was on CNN a lot and I called my wife into the room and told her who he was. How proud I was to think he was from Newburyport! Later I learned that he had written a book called "America the Vulnerable"-- How our government is failing to protect us from Terrorism. I bought it and devoured it in a couple sittings. From the book jacket I learned that Steve is the Jeane J.Kirkpatrick Senior Fellow in National Security Studies at the Council on Foreign Relations. He served in the White House Military Office during the George H. W. Bush administration and was director for Global Issues on the National Security Council staff during the William J. Clinton administration.

All this proves what I wrote at the beginning of this chapter, you never know who is sitting in front of you!

CHAPTER 36
I'll Never Forget the Time I—

—had to sit through drug education for teachers so we could tell the difference between LSD and pot!

—got called to the super's office on the suspension of a teacher.

—totally marked all my midyear exams incorrectly and had to do them all over in one day.

—had to correct my final exams by hand when the Scantron machine broke down.

—brought O'Doul's to school for lunch, thinking it was ginger ale, since they both were in green cans!

—had to deal with the orchestra of a show being totally drunk and playing off key.

—had to console a student in our patriotic pageant when the narrator totally skipped his portrayal of Eisenhower in D-Day.

—was out sick and the administration called to see if I would come in for parents' night that evening.

—was berated by a student for not "giving" him an A instead of only an A-.

—interrupted the contract negotiations and won the ballot count for association president.

—taught my very first class and ran out material after just twenty minutes.

—learned that you can teach but you can learn from your students, too.

—was told not to use red pens to correct anymore, since it upset students too much.

—learned that a teacher killed herself by jumping off a bridge.

—was told by a superintendent that it was blackmail to hold something over his head by revealing it to the staff.

—was informed that school officials didn't know the family status of our students.

—left school early to go to a Clinton for President rally out of state.

—had my car filled with balloons and decorated like a rabbit to celebrate one of my plays' final performance.

—left teaching on my last day and practically ran to my car to get out of the school!

CHAPTER 37
This Side of the Chalkboard

Teaching provided me with an honorable occupation that I loved. I was able to pretty much be my own boss and have summers off. That was a big thing, because I would have gone crazy in a nine-to-five business situation, and the heat just makes me wilt!

Teaching let me shut my door and bring a class of not overly interested or motivated teenagers from point A to point B in forty-five minutes. Later, that got changed to ninety minutes, and then it became apparent that we really were babysitters. Teenagers whose attention span is twenty minutes at best were asked to be engaged for four times that plus.

Teaching let me be my own boss and just put up with observations and evaluations when the spirit moved the administration to justify their jobs—not mine. Who were they going to get to replace me if I got let go? Let's look at what I did in those thirty-seven years.

I taught more than 100 students a year for 37 years, so that is more than 3,700 kids I met in the classroom. It does not account for the 1,000 or so more that I met in drama productions, student councils, yearbook staffs, or Close Up trips to Washington, D.C. These are great education trips run by a fantastic organization and does just what its name says- get sthe students to see their government Close Up! I taught thirty-three different courses over those years, if you take into account all the changes in history and all the levels like honors, standard, and special education classes I had. Social studies has the biggest array of subjects of any high school discipline.

At one point, I was teaching totally out of contract for a number of years with theatre arts classes added to my social studies courses. I sat on a number of committees, from Honors and Eligibility to School and Community for accreditation purposes every decade I taught, and I taught in five decades. I did my duties, like cafeteria duty, study-hall monitoring, and hall duty, for example. Over the years, these have since been negotiated out of the teachers' contracts. I should not forget homeroom, which I had for thirty years, despite being out of contract all those years.

Teaching for me was exciting and interesting. I never forgot my first superintendent's advice in 1965 to be interesting if you teach history. If I didn't like to teach something, why would my students like to learn it, I figured. I lectured and had discussions. I worked in audio/visual things early on and thought it was vital, especially to history. Once I had students listen to Winston Churchill's speeches and later used filmstrips for the same thing. The advent of videotapes was a godsend to me. I really lived up to the old adage that the teacher is given "chicken shit and make chicken salad" out of it with the classes they have.

I had drive and perseverance. I made a career out of teaching, and there was never any other occupation I would have preferred. Today's teachers have all the answers, but I hope they have the stamina my colleagues and I had who started in the 1960s. These people are unique and certainly of the new wave. They don't see why we did things as we did them, but pound their heads against the wall rather than ask for help. Take, for instance, the younger-than-me teacher who used to test her students on material the very last day of the semester, then give a midyear exam as well the next week. There was something wrong here. I told her to include the last material on the midyear and make it easier on herself. She usually had trouble doing her semester grades also, because she let so much go until the very end. If you haven't taught it by the last week, then you have waited too long to teach it. That last week could have been used to review for midyear exams; that would have made it easier on her, and served as a stimulus for the students to know what to study for in conjunction with the upcoming midyear exams.

We loved to teach. We liked each other. We got along and helped each other. We were there for the kids and we were there for each other. My colleagues, at least in social studies, never bickered or backstabbed one another. We were indeed very fortunate to have great department chairmen who were there fighting for us all, rather than for personal gain with the administration.

I had no desire to be anything but a teacher. Once, I was chosen to be an administrative intern and despised it totally. I wanted to teach kids and not be a leader of adults; that is the reason I went into teaching in the first place. Today, when a person comes from the ranks of teaching and is made an administrator, he or she forgets where his or her roots were. I firmly believe that every administrator should teach at least one course every year. Otherwise, they get "fat and flabby" regarding what is happening in the core of education—the classroom. No one should totally leave the classroom, whether principal or superintendent. They must keep their hand in to know what is going on. They do not understand how much education has changed unless they teach—period.

When I became president of my teachers association, I learned a great deal about the profession that I never would have known otherwise. I felt totally helpless at times because of the lack of cooperation of the administration and school committee to deal with teachers as equals. They loved power and control, and got into big trouble for their inflexibility. They don't get it that if they work with the teachers, they can get a better product. They always stay an arm's length away and think that is the way to do it. They can't relax because they think it will make them appear weak.

Teachers are working daily with the worst set of circumstances anyone could ever imagine. For instance, to have a classroom where one couldn't even regulate the heat would not be tolerated for one minute in industry. The business world night be shut down and the people sent home. Yet teachers put up with it and got along to get along. They should be able to walk out. They should be able to suspend a student without going to the administration. The teachers could easily run the schools very well without a principal. If you like bureaucracy, you need principals. If you think the kids and teachers in the classroom are the crux of the matter in public education, then ax the principal. The money saved would be better spent in the classroom. Of the five principals and two interim principals I was under, only one was really with it and worth whatever the school committee was paying him.

We, as teachers, make it look too easy. We are always there and ready to roll. When I invited guest speakers into my classes, it was always eye-opening for them and my students. Once I invited a stockbroker to explain the market to my economics class. She was truly a brilliant person, but she was way over their heads, trying to explain what she did and the process involved. About midway through her lesson, I could see the eyes begin to glass over and I knew we were in big trouble.

Another time, I had a state representative in to talk about his role as our district's lawmaker. We had just converted our schedule to ninety-minute classes, and as the representative progressed at a rapid rate, he had obviously run out of material, and the class was far from over. At the normal time of forty-five minutes, he got set to leave, and I told him that he still had forty-five minutes more to go. He was thunderstruck! I explained that this was what he voted for when he backed the time-on-learning plank of this latest state education law. He told me in no uncertain terms that ninety-minute classes were not what the legislators had in mind to achieve their objective. I told him, "Well, that's what we got!" He shook his head in disbelief when I said yes, when he asked me if I did this every day! We salvaged the day by opening up the remaining time to a question-and-answer session.

Teachers must take the lead in what they know is best for the classroom. I did a number of times during the tenure of thirty-seven years, like the time I got the grant to install the law course in our curriculum. I had gone to a conference and learned about the total disregard the drug culture was teaching the young generation. I thought that if we had law as part of our curriculum, the kids might stop and think before they totally dismantled the "establishment." I approached the superintendent and got permission to take the law course offered by Tufts University in Medford, Massachusetts as part of their Lincoln Filene Center. Four of us went once a week to their course in the evening, and the following semester had the background to teach the program.

It had great effect on our kids, and at least they saw us trying to understand their needs in this new world they were thrown into. We kept the program intact for a number of years, until the state overhauled the social studies curriculum with a concentration on history, and the law course was eliminated. Relevance was the word of the day, and the law course provided that, until someone said otherwise. A quick look at the police blotter in the local paper showed that crime was up, and total disregard for law-enforcement officials was at an all-time high after we got rid of the law course in our curriculum.

Today, much too much is being demanded of teachers everywhere. We were all hired to teach, but we are spending a great deal of our time every day dealing with other stuff. The parents and the public want so much from teachers that they could very easily provide themselves, but instead would rather have the schools deal with it. Schools cannot reform a kid who has been totally abused by his parents. Parents need to be parents. As one parent said to me at one parents' night, "I don't want him to get mad at me!" This was after I asked why this parent didn't provide exactly what he was demanding me to do as his teacher!

Teaching is not for sissies. Teachers are there every day, plugging away the best they can, usually under less-than-ideal conditions. For an administrator to come in once or twice and judge a teacher's career by those few occasions is so totally unprofessional, it is ridiculous. However, teachers have allowed it, and we all know we get what we allow.

Teachers must be leaders and stick to their agenda. They know what is best for the kids—no one else. They have gone to college and entered a noble profession. They have to be able to plow ahead every day, even though they will never be fully appreciated for what they do. By this I mean that teachers have the future in front of them, full of uncertainty and full of such great hope. In high school today, it is sad that many students just want out and have closed minds about life. As I told my students many times, if they were that closed-minded at seventeen or eighteen, what would they be like when they become adults?

The world is changing, and these kids must run it—ready or not! The teachers they have would be fortunate if they were as dedicated, enthusiastic, and committed as the generation I taught with, but I tend to think that they won't be because of the great pressures being exerted on them from the outside world, and from their unwillingness to listen and seek us out. I wish them well, and I leave them with not one regret of anything I did before I retired. Thirty-seven years is a blink of an eye as I look back, but going through it, it certainly was something else. Something no one will ever experience like I did unless they become a public school teacher at the high-school level.

Once a teacher, always a teacher. It's easy to take the teacher out of the school, but it is very difficult to take the school of the teacher. I will always be a champion of correct spelling, and will forever be ready to correct kids for wrongdoing. No matter the time or generation, teaching is a great profession! We need people in contact with young people to show them the way regardless of the computer hardware and all its bells & whistles. The bottom line is that schools provide a fabulous service to society. We will always need them and good teachers to instruct in

143

them. Despite all the problems, the final analysis is that it's the kids who are important, They need inspirational teachers, creative teachers, hard-working teachers, decently paid teachers, enthusiastic teachers who will find something in each student to bring out and educate.

Some other way besides the property tax must be found to pay for public education. This country needs to wake up and provide the funds nationally, to be distributed statewide and dispensed locally so that future generations can have the time of their life like I did and teach for the love of teaching.

All of a Sudden We're Old!

Years ago when the Beatles sang-
"When I get old, losing my hair,
Many years from now
Will you still need me?
Will you still feed me?
When I'm sixty-four?"

I never dreamed that one day it would apply to me! Starting my fourth year of retirement and turning sixty-four , I became fully aware that "golden age", "senior citizen" and "elder" all of a sudden referred to me.

I welcome senior discount prices at the movies, Disney World and football games but still chuckle at how fast my generation is rapidly becoming old. My friends are having all sorts of aliments and operations, that my mother had when she was alive. We are yesterday's news and ex-faculty members. Our love of teaching and spending our entire careers in the profession is something today's younger educators cannot relate to at all. We were a generation inspired by John F. Kennedy when he said, "Ask not what your country can do for you, ask what you can do for your country."

We walked into the classroom and never left. We chalked our way through the Vietnam War, the drug culture, political assassinations, riots and turmoil and came back for more each fall. We admired and emulated the older teachers and loved working with them. We had fun with the kids and enjoyed inspiring them to do well and to let us know how they made out in life. When early retirement, however, was finally passed, we left in droves to enjoy ourselves. We had earned it and deserved it.

We now tire more easily and wonder how we did it each and every day, rising at 5:30 am and going to bed by 10 pm, only to repeat it all over again, year in, year out for thirty-five plus years on the average. We were nuts, but we didn't know it! We had no time to demand more money and better conditions. We just put up with it!

We accomplished a list of 20 - 30 things every day and now are happy to get tow or three things done before sunset. We seek out early bird specials and over fifty-five communities to live in. We ask for the "no smoking" section in restaurants and sometimes the "no kids" section! We wave at the school busses as they pass and thank God we aren't expected to tend to the contents therein.

We know all the answers but nobody's asking. We have valuable experience that they couldn't wait for us to take with us when we left. Advil for arthritis and Ben-gay for pain is purchased by us, not our parents. We have closets full of sweaters we don't wear in Florida and several winter coats that we never put an arm into anymore. Old cassette tapes have given way to CD's and old VCR's have been replaced by DVD's. We can't program cell phones and cringe when they ring. "Is it mine?" "Can you hear me now?"

Pants don't fit at the waistlines that used to be around thirty-six or something. Getting over a cold or having a cut heal takes weeks, not days. We scour the obit page in the paper the way we used to pursue the sports pages. We don't know the names of the kids on the sports teams anymore, but we still root for a Clipper victory.

Are we bellyaching? Are we sorry? No way! We don't have the administration to deal with any longer. We aren't teaching to the MCAS. We can do lunch anytime we want and NOT 10:30 in the morning like we did in school. We don't need a numbered parking space or an identify tag to wear in school. We can enjoy life with no guilty and don't need to leave plans if we can't make it in!

We remember wonderful, sunny fall days in which to teach. We loved it when kids got an A on a test, improving from the C they got on the previous one. We loved the old-fashioned mimeograph and the smell of the duplicating fluid. We had a great time and now have a new chapter in our lives to live. It is different and it is interesting. And, as I say much more now, "It just takes me longer since I'm not thirty-five anymore!"

ABOUT THE AUTHOR

Richard Doyle is a native of Newburyport, Massachusetts. He taught at Newburyport High School for close to 37 years , teaching over a dozen different social studies and theater arts courses and producing & directing 25 plays & musicals as well as serving as faculty advisor to yearbook and student government groups during that time. For the last four years of his teaching career, he was President of the Newburyport Teachers Association.

Doyle's schooling includes Cambridge Junior College, Keene State College and Fitchburg State College. He enjoys watercolor painting, theater, traveling, volunteering for retired teacher associations & museum work. He writes a column for a local paper periodically. With his wife, he divides his time between New Hampshire and Florida having retired from public education in 2002.